LUCENT LIBRARY *of* HISTORICAL ERAS

SCIENCE, TECHNOLOGY, AND WARFARE OF ANCIENT MESOPOTAMIA

LUCENT LIBRARY *of* HISTORICAL ERAS

SCIENCE, TECHNOLOGY, AND WARFARE OF ANCIENT MESOPOTAMIA

DON NARDO

LUCENT BOOKS

A part of Gale, Cengage Learning

GALE
CENGAGE Learning™

Detroit • New York • San Francisco • New Haven, Conn • Waterville, Maine • London

LIBRARY OF CONGRESS CATALOGING-IN-PUBLICATION DATA

Nardo, Don, 1947–
Science, technology, and warfare of ancient Mesopotamia / by Don Nardo.
  p. cm. — (Lucent library of historical eras)
 Includes bibliographical references and index.
 ISBN 978-1-4205-0102-5 (hbk.)
 1. Technology—Iraq—History—To 634—Juvenile literature. 2. Military art and science—Iraq—History—To 634—Juvenile literature. 3. Iraq—Civilization—To 634—Juvenile literature. I. Title.
 T27.I72.S35 2008
 609.35—dc22

                                                          2008026588

Lucent Books
27500 Drake Rd.
Farmington Hills, MI 48331

ISBN-13: 978-1-4205-0102-5
ISBN-10: 1-4205-0102-X

Printed in the United States of America
2 3 4 5 6 7 12 11 10 09

Contents

Foreword

Looking back from the vantage point of the present, history can be viewed as a myriad of intertwining roads paved by human events. Some paths stand out—broad highways whose mileposts, even from a distance of centuries, are clear. The events that propelled the rise to power of Germany's Third Reich, its role in World War II, and its eventual demise, for example, are well defined and documented.

Other roads are less distinct, their route sometimes hidden from view. Modern legislatures may have developed from old tribal councils, for example, but the links between them are indistinct in places, open to discussion and interpretation.

The architecture of civilization—law, religion, art, science, and government—as well as the more everyday aspects of our culture—what we eat, what we wear—all developed along the historical roads and byways. In that progression can be traced every facet of modern life.

A broad look back along these roads reveals that many paths—though of vastly different character—seem to converge at a few critical junctions. These intersections are those great historical eras that echo over the long, steady course of human history, extending beyond the past and into the present.

These epic periods of time are the focus of Historical Eras. They shine through the mists of history like beacons, illuminated by a burst of creativity that propels events forward—so bright that we, from thousands of years away, can clearly see the chain of events leading to the present.

Each Historical Eras consists of a set of books that highlight various aspects of these major eras. For example, the Elizabethan England library features volumes on Queen Elizabeth I and her court, Elizabethan theater, the great playwrights, and everyday life in Elizabethan London.

The mini-library approach allows for the division of each era into its most significant and most interesting parts and the exploration of those parts in depth. Also, social and cultural trends as well as illustrative documents and eyewitness accounts can be prominently featured in individual volumes.

Historical Eras presents a wealth of information to young readers. The lively narrative, fully documented primary and secondary source quotations, maps, photographs, sidebars, and annotated bibliographies serve as launching points for class discussion and further research.

In studying the great historical eras, students also develop a better understanding of our own times. What we learn from the past and how we apply it in the present may shape the future and may determine whether our era will be a guiding light to those traveling future roads.

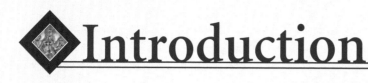
SIMPLE BUT REVOLUTIONARY TECHNOLOGY

In early modern times, the peoples and tribal groups of the Middle East possessed little in the way of advanced science and technology. There were few paved roads and bridges in the region, few cars or other motorized vehicles, few factories, few doctors trained in modern medical techniques, no astronomical observatories, and no university courses in modern science, engineering, or medicine. At the time, these advances existed only in more advanced Western nations, including Britain, France, Germany, and the United States.

In fact, such differences between "West" and "East" profoundly shaped relations between the two groups. The relative technological backwardness of the Middle East was a major reason why Western nations were long able to exploit the region. In the 1920s, shortly after World War I, for instance, the British sought to control the vast oil reserves in Iraq, the region that had encompassed Mesopotamia in ancient times. Even after Iraq became an independent country in 1932, Britain maintained troops and technical advisers there for several years. In part, this was to help the Iraqis learn to adopt and use Western technology; but it was also a way to allow the British to continue benefiting from the region's plentiful, and at the time inexpensive, oil.

Ancient Sumer: Land of Many "Firsts"

What most of the people involved, British and Iraqis alike, did not know was that in the distant past, the technological balance had been quite different. In ancient times, the Near East (the term scholars use for the Middle East before the modern era) and especially Mesopotamia were at the cutting edge, so to speak, of human civilization. It was on the plains of southern Mesopotamia that the Sumerians built the world's first cities and invented writing. They were also the first to use what is today viewed as basic technology. The city-dwelling Sumerians were erecting multistoried temples, smelting metals for tools and weapons, and using the wheel in transportation and industry at the time when the inhabitants of Europe were still living in ancient villages and using stone tools and weapons.

Indeed, the Sumerians were responsible for dozens of other "firsts." In his now classic book *History Begins at Sumer,* the late, great scholar Samuel N. Kramer lists many of them. Some, he writes, were literary, such as the first epic poems, proverbs, almanac, and lullaby. Others were social and cultural, such as the first schools, libraries, laws, and legal ideas.

Kramer also points out that the scientific disciplines of cosmology and cosmogony appeared for the first time in ancient Mesopotamia. Cosmology is the study of the universe (all that exists), its structure, and humanity's place within it. Cosmogony, by contrast, seeks to understand the origins of the universe and the world (and, by extension, humanity). The Sumerians, Babylonians, and other inhabitants of Mesopotamia, Kramer writes, speculated

This map shows the region of Mesopotamia and the Fertile Crescent.

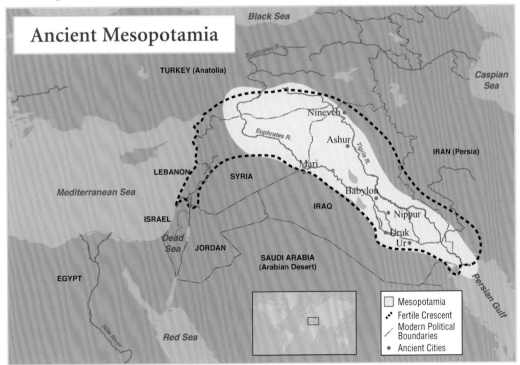

A tablet from Mesopotamia dated to 3000 B.C. contains pictographs representing an early form of writing. The invention of writing is credited to the Sumerians, whose civilization produced many other literary, social, and cultural "firsts."

on the nature and, more particularly, the origin of the universe, and on its method of operation. There is good reason to infer that in the third millennium B.C. there emerged a group of Sumerian thinkers and teachers who, in their quest for satisfactory answers to some of the problems raised by their cosmic speculations, evolved a cosmology and theology carrying such high intellectual conviction that their doctrines became the basic creed and dogma of much of the ancient Near East.[1]

True, this "creed and dogma" that Kramer mentions was not scientific in the modern sense. Science, as we know it today, utilizes the scientific method, in which ideas and theories are based on evidence that can be measured. Moreover, the introduction of new evidence regularly proves older theories wrong. Sumerian thinkers, Kramer points out, "failed to discover that all-important intellectual tool which we take for granted: the scientific method . . . without which our present-day science would never have reached its prominence."[2] Thus, the first use of true science must be credited to the Greeks in the mid-first millennium B.C., long after Sumerian civilization had declined.

Cultural Borrowings

Nevertheless, the Greeks often based their scientific notions on ideas borrowed from the Near East, particularly Babylonia. (Babylonia reached its cultural height at about the same time that the earliest Greek scientists appeared.) The Babylonians developed a complex mathematical system. And they applied it to their studies of the heavens by dividing the sky into units, now called degrees, minutes, and seconds. They also designated certain key star groups, or constellations (including those of the zodiac), that people in later cultures and eras kept and still recognize today. And they kept regular records of the movements of the heavenly bodies and compiled large archives of observations made over the course of many centuries. Thus, the Greeks owed, and modern astronomers still owe, much to their Babylonian predecessors.

Likewise, ancient Mesopotamian medicine was backward by modern standards. Much of it was based on the idea that illness is caused by evil spirits inhabiting the body. Yet a number of Babylonian and other Mesopotamian doctors took a serious, practical approach to healing. Although they did not understand what causes disease, they developed some basic techniques that paved the way for Hippocrates, the Greek now called "the Father of Medicine."

In addition, the Mesopotamian development of the wheel, metal weapons, the chariot, advanced bows, siege devices, and other aspects of physical technology transformed warfare in the ancient world. These aspects of technology not only made fighting more lethal and conquest more common in the Near East, but they also filtered outward into other regions. Not long after the lightweight chariot appeared in Mesopotamia in the early second millennium B.C., for example, it spread to Egypt and eventually to parts of southeastern Europe, including Greece.

Slow to Change

Two general points can be made about these and other aspects of ancient Mesopotamian science and technology. First, most were simple, even rudimentary, compared to the complex machines created by modern science and technology. The wooden plow, for instance, may not be so impressive today, in a world in which farmers regularly use sophisticated tractors and harvesters having hundreds or thousands of moving parts. Yet long ago, that humble plow revolutionized the Near East and the world. It made it possible for early farmers to produce much larger quantities of food, which in turn stimulated local population growth and eventually led to cities and urbanization.

Second, the pace of scientific and technological change was extremely slow in ancient times, particularly as compared to today. As noted University of Oklahoma scholar Daniel C. Snell puts it, "There is

A tablet containing a geometry problem and figures was created in Babylonia around 1750 B.C. Babylonian advances in mathematics influenced their study of astronomy, which was then furthered by the ancient Greeks.

a discontinuity between our own societies, in which technological change affects everything rapidly, and earlier societies, in which such change was slower."[3] The slowness was often the result of respect for tradition and the status quo or the belief that existing methods were perfectly satisfactory. This is one reason why the ancient Mesopotamians never developed complex laborsaving devices, such as tractors. Abundant, cheap manual labor was readily available in the form of millions of poor peasants. So why invent something that would put most of them out of work? In reading about the development of Mesopotamian science and technology, therefore, one must keep in mind that the people who used it saw the world and their place within it much differently than we do today.

Chapter One

ASTRONOMY, MATH, AND MEASUREMENT

When the ancient Mesopotamians gazed up at the night sky, they beheld a sight witnessed by few people in today's industrialized societies. In those days, there was no smog or other air pollution. Nor was there light pollution from bright city lights. These factors often wash out most of the stars and other objects in modern night skies so that only the brightest ones are visible, and those only dimly.

In contrast, on cloudless nights (which were few in the region) the Sumerians, Babylonians, and other residents of Mesopotamia looked up to see an immense, inky-black canopy. Imbedded within it was a spectacular array of thousands of stationary stars. Also visible were five very bright, slowly moving planets: Mercury, Venus, Mars, Jupiter, and Saturn. (Uranus and Neptune are too dim to see without a telescope, and people in those days did not realize that Earth is a planet.)

Exactly what these luminous objects studding the night sky were, no one knew for sure. But they developed theories that tied them into their religious beliefs, whereby the planets were associated with specific gods. Because the heavenly deities affected life on Earth, or so it was thought, then the planets must also have a bearing on human activities.

Because of this religious dimension, Mesopotamian astronomy was not science in the modern sense, as University of Windsor scholar Stephen Bertman explains:

The priests of Mesopotamia viewed astronomy not as an end in itself, but as a means to a higher spiritual truth. Their concern for most of their history was not with astronomy as a science but with astrology as an art by which the future could be divined through the discovery of omens, good and bad, to inform political decision making and assure personal success.[4]

Despite these nonscientific aspects of Mesopotamian astronomy/astrology, the chief skygazers, especially among the Babylonians, did eventually establish certain basic scientific principles and practices. They kept careful records of planetary movements, for instance. They also developed a logical, sound mathematical system to measure the sky. And they expanded this system and applied it to everyday life, including measuring land parcels and weighing commodities in the marketplace.

Observing the Heavens

All of the peoples who lived in ancient Mesopotamian made regular observations of the night sky. But the Babylonians,

A Babylonian astrological calendar from the first millennium B.C. reveals that the study of the heavens was both a scientific and a spiritual effort in ancient Mesopotamia.

Assyrians, and Persians were particularly eager stargazers who used painstaking, sometimes ingenious methods. Their astronomers used hollow tubes as view-finders. They also used water clocks to time the risings and settings of stars and planets. Other celestial (heavenly) phenomena observed and duly noted included Venus's disappearance behind the Sun and subsequent reappearance; the occasional retrograde (backward) movement of some planets; and the occasional appearance of eclipses, comets, halos of light around the Moon or Sun, and so forth.

The astronomers recorded their timings and measurements on clay tablets, which they deposited in archives (libraries), usually located in palaces or temples. The earliest surviving examples date from about 1700 B.C. Of particular interest and importance to modern scholars are the so-called "Venus tablets," assembled by the astronomers of the Babylonian king Ammi-saduqa (reigned 1646–1626 B.C.). The data found on the tablets was originally intended to reveal clues to the king's fate. But today these observations are useful in dating ancient Mesopotamian events.

Although unusual celestial events, such as eclipses, were noteworthy as potential omens that might affect the king or nation, observations of more ordinary solar, lunar, and planetary movements were also viewed as important. This is because they helped the peoples of the region create calendars to keep track of the months and years. Repeated observations of the Moon's movements, for example, resulted in a fairly accurate

lunar calendar by the seventh century B.C. It divided the year into twelve lunar months. As time went on, each month came to be associated with one of the twelve star groups, or constellations, collectively called the zodiac. During the period in which the Greek Seleucid Empire controlled Mesopotamia (the late first millennium B.C.), horoscopes based on the signs of the zodiac appeared. Versions of these are still popular today.

The division of the year into twelve lunar months did have one glaring problem, however. As noted scholar Gwendolyn Leick points out, the Babylonians' solution to this problem reflected their peculiar thought processes and worldview:

The twelve lunar months make 354 days. This left a shortage of some twelve days for the solar year [of a bit more than 365 days]. The Babylonian solution was to adhere to the regular and ideal lunar "year" but periodically . . . add a thirteenth "exceptional" month, which was decreed by the king upon lengthy consultation by his diviners [priests who interpreted divinely inspired signs]. This attitude of always assuming a regular measurement [in spite of the] irregularities of actual events was most characteristic for the Babylonian mentality. [It] affected the whole society, [as it] was intimately linked to an intellectual tradition of thousands of years. It was one of the manifestations of "wisdom" which was divine in origin.[5]

How Ancient Astronomy Helps Historians

Babylonian observations of the heavens are important not only because of their historical value as precursors to science but also because they help modern historians date ancient events. Particularly valuable in this regard is the data collected by the royal astronomers of the Babylonian king Ammi-saduqa (reigned 1646–1626 B.C.). These ancient observers closely watched and recorded the risings and settings of the planet Venus, for example. Their intent was to use the data to help predict future events. In contrast, modern scholars use it to help achieve accurate dates for the reigns of the Babylonian rulers in Ammi-saduqa's dynasty. Knowing these dates, they can make educated guesses about the dates of reigns and events before and after that dynasty.

Some scholarly disagreements remain about how to interpret Venus's ancient cycle. But the consensus is that the present dating of Mesopotamian events in the second millennium B.C. is accurate to within a century or so.

A tablet dated from the seventh century B.C. is a copy of a text from about 1,000 years earlier, which recorded observations of the planet Venus. This has helped modern historians estimate the dates of the reigns of rulers from around the time the text was written.

Keeping careful records of the motions of celestial objects also allowed Babylonian astronomers to develop useful units for calculating time, including hours and minutes. They divided an hour into sixty minutes and counted twelve "double hours" in each day. (Greek astronomers later divided these into twenty-four single hours, creating the system familiar today.) The Babylonian version of the solar year became extremely accurate by ancient standards. The fourth-century B.C. astronomer Kidinnu (or Kidenas) measured its length with an error of only about four minutes. (A number of later Greek and Roman scholars, including the Roman encyclopedist Pliny the Elder, mentioned Kidinnu's accomplishments in a favorable light.)

A Math System Still Used Today

Ancient sources say that Kidinnu was a mathematician as well as an astronomer. And indeed, mathematics and astronomy were (as they are today) closely linked in ancient Mesopotamia. In fact, the Sumerians and Babylonians made several crucial contributions to the science of mathematics, some of which are still widely used today.

For example, the Sumerians used a version of the decimal system, based on the number 10. (It appears that they borrowed parts of it from the earlier inhabitants of the region.) It used small clay tokens to indicate various numbers. One token stood for 1 sheep, 1 measure of grain, or, in the more general sense, the number 1. Another token stood for 10 sheep or the number 10. In this system, a number such as 23 was denoted by two number-10 tokens and three number-1 tokens.

At first the tokens were part of a strictly physical exchange between buyers and sellers. But after the Sumerians invented writing in the fourth millennium (the 3000s) B.C., they began recording symbols for tokens and numbers on clay tablets. These signs were at first highly complex. But by the last centuries of the third millennium (the 2000s) B.C., the system had become simpler, with just two symbols—a vertical wedge and a corner wedge. These had numerous different meanings depending on their placement. Written one way, they indicated the number 60 (6×10). Configured another way, they might stand for 3,600 (60×60). All the multiples used either 6 or 10, which made it a kind of sexagesimal system (one based on the number 60).

Later, the Babylonians carried mathematics to a still higher level. As H.W.F. Saggs of the University of Wales puts it:

> No one with any feeling for mathematics can fail to be impressed by the achievements of the Babylonians. . . . The mathematical expertise of some Babylonians of about 1800 B.C., or perhaps their predecessors, exceeded that of most people today, other than those with a degree in mathematics. For example, they had calculated the square root of 2 correct to 1 in two million.[6]

On a simpler level, Babylonian scholars continued to use the Sumerian decimal system for counting. But this was only for numbers from 1 to 59. Beyond these, the Babylonians created a new system that combined elements of decimal and sexagesimal systems. This made it more complex and harder to learn than the strictly decimal system used in most of the world today. For example, if a Babylonian wanted to designate the number 7,664, he or she expressed it as 2,7,44. Reading from right to left, the second number was an order of magnitude higher than the first and the third an order higher than the second. Thus, the user understood that the 2 stood for 2×60^2 (or 7,200), the 7 for 7×60 (or 420), and the 44 for 44 single decimal units. Adding the three numbers together, therefore, produced 7,200 + 420 + 44 = 7,664.

The Babylonian counting system, which regularly used both square and cube roots, was not simply a mathematical theory known only to a few select thinkers. Rather, almost all those who learned to read and write mastered it. Students (mostly in scribal schools) practiced by solving math problems similar to those in modern schoolbooks. Such an exercise has survived:

Problem: If somebody asks you thus: As much as the side of the square

Clay tokens of various sorts were assigned different values and used for accounting in ancient Mesopotamia during the late fourth millennium B.C.

A Mesopotamian Horoscope

The first horoscopes (predictions of how the movements of the heavenly bodies might affect human lives) appeared in Mesopotamia in the fifth century B.C. In the centuries that followed, people often hired astrologers to predict the future of children born on specific dates. One surviving horoscope from that era reads in part:

In the year 48 of the Seleucid era [263 B.C.], on the night of the twenty-third of Adar [February/March], a child was born. At the same time the Sun was 30 degrees into [the constellation] Aries; the Moon 10 degrees into Aquarius; Jupiter at the start of Leo; Venus with the Sun; Mercury with the Sun; Saturn in Cancer; and Mars at Cancer's end. . . . He won't be rich. His appetite won't be satisfied. What he has when he is young, he will lose. But then for 36 years he will prosper, and his life will be long.

Quoted in Stephen Bertman, *Handbook to Life in Ancient Mesopotamia*. New York: Facts On File, 2003, p. 170.

which I made I dug deep, and I extracted one *musaru* [60^3] and a half of volume of earth. My base I made a square. How deep did I go? Solution: You, in your procedure, operate with 12. Take the reciprocal of 12 and multiply by 1,30,0,0 which is your volume. 7,30,0 you will see [i.e., will be the answer]. What is the cube root of 7,30,0? 30 is the cube root. Multiply 30 by 1, and 30 you [will] see. Multiply 30 by another 1, and 30 you [will] see. Multiply 30 by twelve, and 6,0 [360] you [will] see. 30 is the side of your square, and 6,0 [360] is your depth.[7]

Some elements of the Babylonian system have survived. Familiar examples are the division of a circle into 360 degrees and the allotment of 60 seconds to a minute and 60 minutes to an hour in time-keeping and navigation.

The Technology of Weights and Measures

The Sumerian and Babylonian counting systems also became an important cornerstone of standard weights and measures. Financial activities, such as buying and selling, money exchanging, and trade, required such standards to make transactions fair and reliable. Using mathematics to measure land plots, bushels of corn, and so forth was in a way a concrete, technological, and practical expression of theoretical numerical concepts.

It is not surprising that the Sumerians, who introduced the first units of weight and measurement, included many units based on the numbers 6 and 60. "Since the basic mathematical system was sexigesimal," Leick says, "basic units were divided or multiplied in a sexigesimal manner."[8] The Sumerians added other measuring units based on the approximate lengths of the human finger and forearm. Later, the Babylonians and Assyrians kept most of the Sumerian weights and measures, although they sometimes had their own names for them.

For example, the basic early Babylonian unit of weight was the *she* (from the Sumerian *se*). It was equal to 1/600 of a modern ounce (.05g). By the mid-first millennium B.C., the *she* had been replaced by the *shiklu,* later popularly

known as the shekel, equal to 180 *she,* or .3 ounces (9g). This is about the weight of a U.S. quarter. In the system used by the Assyrians and Babylonians, 60 shekels equaled 1 *manu,* and 60 *manu* equaled 1 *biltu,* or roughly 67 pounds (30kg).

Like earlier Sumerian versions, Babylonian units of length and distance were based on finger and forearm lengths. The average forearm length was later widely called a cubit, a term used frequently in the Old Testament, which was written in Mesopotamia and Palestine in the first millennium B.C. One *ubanu,* based on the Sumerian *shu-si,* or "finger," was equivalent to about 2/3 of an inch (about 1.6cm). And 1 *ammatu,* or cubit, was equal to about 15.5 inches (39cm). Large

A set of weights made from hematite dating from 1900 to 1600 B.C. allowed ancient Mesopotamians to accurately and fairly calculate the value of certain goods and objects for financial transactions.

Measuring the Land

The Sumerians were the first Mesopotamians to develop large-scale agriculture. To make it clear exactly how much land a person, temple, or the government owned, they used their knowledge of mathematics to develop units of measure that could be applied to land. These units remained in use later, when the region was under the control of Akkadian speakers (Babylonians and Assyrians), although the names of the units sometimes changed. The Sumerian *sar*, or "garden," for example, became the Akkadian *musaru*, both equal to 27.5 square yards (23sq.m). One Sumerian *iku*, or "field," became an Akkadian *iku*, equaling 100 *musaru*, or 5/6 of an acre (.32ha). And 1 Sumerian *bur* became an Akkadian *buru*, which equaled 18 *iku*, or 15 acres (6ha).

units of measure included the *kanu*, or "cane," equal to 6 *ammatu*, or 7 feet 10 inches (2.3m); the *ashlu*, equal to 157 feet (48m); and the *beru*, or "league," equal to 5.25 miles (8.4km).

Trade, buying, and selling also necessitated standard units of volume. One of the more common was the *sila* (a term used by both the Sumerians and Babylonians), equal to about 1.5 pints (.7L). One *massiktu* equaled 60 *sila*, an amount equivalent to 11 gallons (41.6L) or 1.3 bushels. An average donkey load in ancient Mesopotamia was called an *imeru*, equal to 100 *sila*, or about 2.25 bushels.

When the Babylonians were conquered by the Persians in the sixth century B.C., the Persian government wisely kept most of the Sumerian-Babylonian weights and measures in place. Adopting a radically new system would obviously have caused much confusion and financial disruption.

Some of the Persian units were a bit different from the older ones, however. A Persian finger (*aiwas*), for instance, was .8 inch (2cm); a hand (*dva*) was equal to 5 fingers or 4 inches (10cm); a cubit (*panka*) was 20 inches (50cm); and a *parasang*, the distance a person could walk in an hour at an average pace, was 3.7 miles (6km). Common Persian units of weight were the shekel at .3 ounces (8.3g); the mina, equal to 60 shekels; and the talent, equal to 3,000 shekels.

A generation after the Macedonian Greek king Alexander III (later called "the Great") subdued the Persian Empire in the late fourth century B.C., the Greek Seleucid Empire inherited Mesopotamia. Evidence for the use of weights and measures in this period is sparse. But it appears that the Seleucid rulers kept the older systems in place, favoring some over others in specific areas. In Babylon, for example, people seem to have used the Babylonian system. Not surprisingly, the Seleucids also introduced some Greek units of measure. One of these was the Attic foot (which originated in Athens), measuring 11.6 inches (29cm). Another Greek unit used in parts of Mesopotamia was the stade (or *stadion*), equal to 600 Attic feet.

These and other units of weight and measurement were very much hands-on and useful in everyday life. The residents of ancient Mesopotamia may not have used science in the modern sense, but they did have basic forms of technology, including practical uses for number systems.

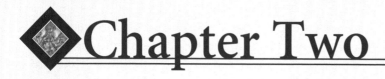
MEDICINE AND DOCTORS

Modern scholars accept that doctors, in the form of healers who used ancient folk remedies, must have existed in Mesopotamia long before the Sumerians created the first cities in the late 3000s B.C. And doctors were certainly an important part of society from that time on. A popular old saying in the region was, "Infection without a doctor is like hunger without food."[9]

Ancient Medical Texts

The first direct evidence for doctors and the practice of medicine in Mesopotamia are written texts in which these healers recorded various illnesses and how to deal with them. The oldest such text that has survived is from the Sumerian city of Nippur and dates to shortly before 3000 B.C. A considerably larger collection of medical texts, consisting of about eight hundred clay tablets, was discovered in the palace library of the Assyrian king Ashurbanipal (reigned ca. 668–627 B.C.) at Nineveh.

These tablets contain numerous references to ancient folk beliefs that today seem strange or even silly. Some offered a prognosis, or a prediction of how a patient's condition would progress, such as, "If the door of the house where the sick man lies gives a cry like a lion, he [the patient] will linger on [in pain] and then die."[10] Cures were also listed. Some were practical, such as inhaling vapors to relieve congestion. Others were more magical in nature, such as sprinkling holy water over a sick person.

The texts also contain references to several hundred substances that were thought to have healing properties. Of these, some came from plants, others from minerals common to Mesopotamia. Noted scholar A. Leo Oppenheim describes some of these substances and how they were used. (He points out that they are similar to folk remedies used later in parts of medieval Europe.)

Native herbs of many kinds; animal products such as fat, tallow, blood, milk, and bones; and a small number of mineral substances. Nothing of notable rarity or expense imported from far-off regions is mentioned [in the texts]. . . . The herbs—roots, stems, leaves, fruits—were used either dry or fresh, ground and sifted, or soaked and boiled. They were mixed with such carriers as beer, vinegar, honey, and tallow. Some were to be swallowed or introduced into the patient's body by means of enemas. . . . Others were to be used on the body directly or in lotions or salves.[11]

Other plant substances and minerals listed in the medical texts include tree bark and gum, seeds, spices (such as thyme and myrrh), castor oil, licorice, potassium nitrate (saltpeter), sodium chloride (salt), and sulfur. In addition to mixing these materials with carrier liquids such as beer or milk or using

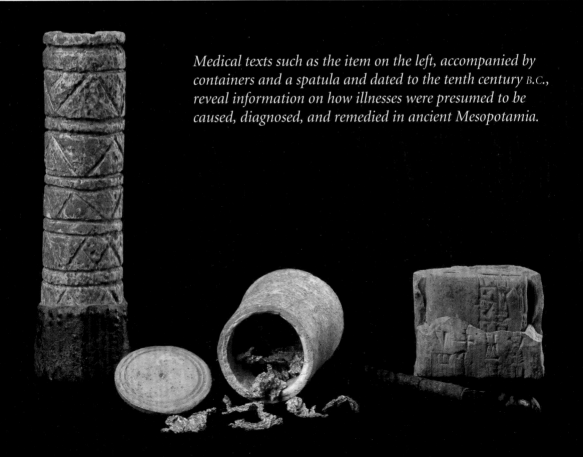

Medical texts such as the item on the left, accompanied by containers and a spatula and dated to the tenth century B.C., reveal information on how illnesses were presumed to be caused, diagnosed, and remedied in ancient Mesopotamia.

them as ointments on the skin, doctors sometimes injected them directly into the eyes, ears, rectum, vagina, or penis.

Doctors and Diagnosis

The doctors who administered the medicinal substances listed in the texts fell into two broad groups or categories. One kind of physician, the *asu,* was a practical healer who relied on these natural substances to help his patients. The other kind of doctor, the *ashipu* (or *asipu*), attempted to heal the sick through spiritual or magical means.

This does not mean, however, that every *ashipu* used only spiritual cures and every *asu* only practical ones. Evidently, some healers were knowledgeable in both disciplines; moreover, sometimes a patient, or the relative of a patient, felt the need to call in two separate "specialists," so to speak. Evidence for this takes the form of a surviving Assyrian letter that states, "Let him appoint one *ashipu* and one *asu,* and let them perform their treatment together on my behalf."[12]

Mesopotamian doctors must have been proud of their profession, as they adopted a specific symbol to identify and advertise both the profession and themselves. The symbol consisted of a staff with snakes encircling it. This image was later adopted by ancient Greek physicians and later still by modern ones. Like the

division of a circle into 360 degrees, this is another way that the region's ancient cultures contributed to the later development of science.

Sumerian, Babylonian, and other ancient Mesopotamian doctors frequently tended to their patients on the grounds of religious temples. As a result, some temples were thought of as medical clinics as well as places of worship. (A similar association of temples with healing developed in ancient Greece.) The doctors arrived at the temples (or private houses if they were making house calls) carrying bags filled with medicines, bandages, and other medical items. We know this thanks to a surviving religious text dedicated to Gula, the Babylonian goddess of healing. In the guise of a doctor, she states, "I am a physician. I know how to heal. I carry with me all the herbs. . . . I am provided with a bag full of effective [cures]. I carry [medical] texts for healing. I effect cures for all."[13]

Some of the surviving Mesopotamian medical texts show how the doctors diagnosed and treated various diseases and conditions. These included smallpox, typhus, bubonic plague, gout, gonorrhea, tuberculosis, epilepsy, colic, diarrhea, and various intestinal problems. Another condition commonly treated was jaundice, a yellowish discoloration of the skin caused by a chemical imbalance in the blood. Appropriately, they

Community Medicine for the Poor?

The fifth-century B.C. Greek historian Herodotus visited Mesopotamia and later recorded some of the local customs in his now famous history book. He seems to have been confused because he claimed there were no doctors in the region. The custom he describes in the following passage may be accurate but may reflect the situation only in poor villages or neighborhoods, where people could not afford professional medical help and resorted instead to a sort of community medicine.

[T]hey] bring their invalids out into the street, where anyone who comes along offers the sufferer advice on his complaint, either from personal experience or observation of a similar complaint in others. Anyone will stop by the sick man's side and suggest remedies which he has himself proved successful. ... Nobody is allowed to pass a sick person in silence; but everyone must ask him what is the matter.

Herodotus, *The Histories*, trans. Aubrey de Sélincourt. New York: Penguin, 2003, p. 121.

called it the "yellow disease." One text gives this diagnosis: "If a man's body is yellow, his face is yellow, and his eyes are yellow, and the flesh is flabby, it is the yellow disease."[14] Mesopotamian physicians also recognized some forms of mental illness, though clearly they did not properly understand what caused them.

Causes of Illness

Sadly, in fact, Babylonian and other Mesopotamian doctors had no clue to the real causes of the vast majority of physical and mental ailments. They had no inkling of the existence of germs, for example, since the invention of the microscope lay thousands of years in the future. (The germ theory of disease was not formally proposed and proven until the 1800s.)

Yet healers and most others in ancient Mesopotamia were neither stupid nor unobservant. They were well aware that certain diseases could be passed from person to person and, therefore, in such cases it was helpful to limit a sick person's contact with other people. A surviving letter written by Zimri-Lim, an eighteenth-century B.C. king of Mari (on the upper Euphrates), makes this quite clear:

I have heard that the lady Nanname has been taken ill. She has many contacts with the people of the palace. She meets many ladies in her house. Now then, give severe orders that no one should drink [from] the cup [from which] she drinks, no one should sit on the seat where she sits, no one should sleep in the bed where she sleeps. She should no longer meet any ladies in her house. This disease is contagious.[15]

Exactly how people at that time viewed contagion and its workings is unknown. Probably they assumed that, like most kinds of illness, it was caused by evil spirits or demons sent by the gods to punish humans. (This was a major difference between Mesopotamian doctors and Greek physicians. The Greeks eventually gave up the notion that disease is a divine punishment and pioneered the modern view—that illness has purely natural causes.) As for these evil spirits and demons, Mesopotamian medicine recognized as many as six thousand separate ones. Each was thought to be responsible for a specific ailment. It was part of a doctor's task to identify which demon was making his patient sick. The belief was that the demon inhabiting the patient was punishing the person for some kind of sin. So doctors saw it as their duty to perform those religious rituals that tradition indicated would counteract the evil being's bad effects.

In some undetermined percentage of cases, the doctor felt that performing an exorcism (driving the demon from the patient's body) was necessary. The exact way in which such rituals occurred is unknown. But evidence for some of the steps involved has survived in a tablet dating to the seventh century B.C. The Assyrian monarch Esarhaddon (ca. 680–669 B.C.) was ill, and one of his royal diviners told him the following:

As to Your Majesty's writing to me concerning the ritual, they should perform the exorcistic ritual [to expel the sickness-causing demon] exactly as Your Majesty did several times already. As to [the] formulas [spells] to be pronounced, the king

An amulet dated from the first millennium B.C. depicts Lamashtu, a female demon who was thought to have caused puerperal fever. Ancient Mesopotamians presumed that illness was caused by evil spirits and demons and could thus be cured by religious rituals and exorcisms.

should watch the formulas carefully. The king should not eat what has been cooked on fire; he should put on a loose robe of a nurse; the day after tomorrow he should go down to the river to wash himself. The king should perform these [rituals] several times.[16]

Yet although evil spirits were seen as the most prevalent cause of disease and illness, Mesopotamian doctors did recognize a few natural causes. They realized that exposure to too much heat or too much cold could make a person sick, for instance. They also saw that overeating, eating spoiled food, and drinking too much alcohol could make someone unwell. In such cases, the doctor's job was fairly easy—simply to advise the patient to eat and drink in moderation.

Surgery and Dentistry

Some Mesopotamian doctors also performed surgery, although very little specific information about actual operations has survived. Some evidence suggests that they did trepanations, procedures in which sections of the scalp and skull bone were removed, exposing part of the brain. Evidently, trepanation was used to treat skull fractures, severe headaches, and epilepsy. Also, it appears that tumors were removed from people's eyes. And castration (removal of the male sex organs) seems to have been performed often on men who attended or had access to royal harems (so that they could not have sex with the king's wives).

Whatever operations were performed in ancient Mesopotamia, there is no doubt that surgery was partly guided by

Beware the Black Dog

A large number of the surviving medical texts from ancient Mesopotamia deal with the work of spiritual doctors (*ashipu*), including exorcisms. Traditional formulas (repeated words and phrases) were developed for these texts. One common one began, "If the exorcist is going to the house of a patient . . . ," and it was followed by a possible omen (divine sign) that the healer might see on his way to the house. As the following examples show,

it was thought that certain omens could determine the course of the patient's illness: "If the exorcist sees either a black dog or a black pig, that sick man will die. If the exorcist sees a white pig, that sick man will live. If the exorcist sees pigs which keep lifting up their tails, that sick man [will not suffer from] anxiety."

Quoted in H.W.F. Saggs, *The Greatness That Was Babylon.* New York: New American Library, 1968, p. 435.

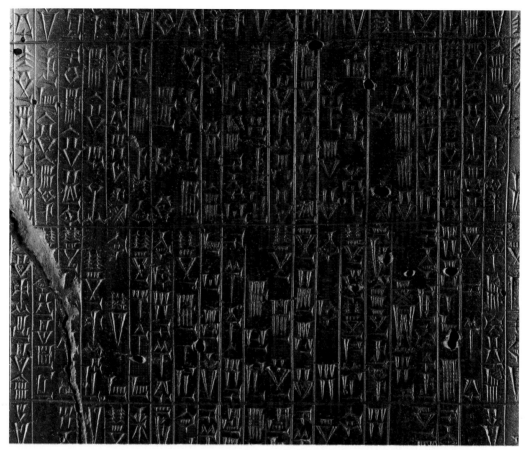

Among the laws cited in the code of Babylonian king Hammurabi, written in the eighteenth century B.C., are those that cover the fees that surgeons could charge for their services, as well as the penalties issued when treatment failed or malpractice was suspected. Shown here is a small sample from the complete text of the code.

legal concepts, including malpractice, just as modern surgery is. The region's law codes, notably that of the Babylonian king Hammurabi (ca. 1792–1750 B.C.), set fees for surgical procedures and recorded the penalties doctors suffered if their surgeries failed. By law, the amount a doctor could charge for his services depended on the patient's ability to pay. The law regulating surgery on a noble states, "If a physician makes a large incision with an operating knife and cures it, or if he opens a tumor over the eye with an operating knife, and saves the eye, he shall receive ten shekels in money." In contrast, an ordinary person had to pay the surgeon only half as much as the noble did. A slave paid less than half of what a commoner paid: "If he [the patient] be the slave of someone,

Learning by Observation

Although many Mesopotamian doctors relied on spiritual formulas and magic to determine what ailed their patients, some learned by simple observation. They saw that certain symptoms led to specific outcomes in most cases. Thus, although the prognosis (prediction of how the patient will fare) that came from these observations was not always accurate, more often than not it was. The following examples, taken from surviving medical texts, deal with pregnant women.

If the pregnant woman repeatedly vomits, she will not go full term. If blood comes from the pregnant woman's mouth, she will not survive childbed. If the pregnant woman discharges [pus] from her mouth, she will die, together with that which is within her womb.

Quoted in H.W.F. Saggs, *Civilization Before Greece and Rome.* New Haven, CT: Yale University Press, 1991, p. 261.

his owner shall give the physician two shekels."[17]

As for penalties for malpractice, a surgeon who caused the death of a noble was in serious trouble. According to law, "If a physician makes a large incision with the operating knife, and kills him, or opens a tumor with the operating knife, and cuts out the eye, his hands shall be cut off."[18]

Some doctors also performed surgery on animals. This made them the earliest known versions of veterinarians. The evidence for them appears in another of Hammurabi's laws: "If a veterinary surgeon performs a serious operation on an ass or an ox, and cures it, the owner shall pay the surgeon one-sixth of a shekel as a fee."[19]

Ancient texts also mention the existence of Mesopotamian dentists. However, it is unlikely that they were doctors trained in a separate medical discipline, as modern dentists are. At the time, the belief was that tooth decay was caused by a hideous worm born in a rotting swamp that formed during Earth's creation. The myth telling how the gods allowed the worm to infect people's teeth went as follows:

The worm went, weeping, before [the sun god,] Shamash, his tears flowing before Ea [god of fresh water]. "What will you give me for food? What will you give me to suck on?" [Shamash answered,] "I will give you the ripe fig and the apricot." [The worm asked,] "What good is the ripe fig and the apricot? Lift me up, and assign me to the teeth and the gums! I will suck the blood of the tooth, and I will gnaw its roots at the gum!" Because you have said this, O worm, may Ea strike you with the might of his hand![20]

The believed causes of tooth decay aside, removal of an infected tooth was an unpleasant experience to say the least. There was no Novocain or laughing gas to dull the pain. The doctor simply grasped the tooth with a metal instrument similar to pliers, cursed the worm three times in a row, and then yanked with all his might. He then told the patient to rinse several times a day with a mouthwash made of beer and sesame seed oil.

Progress Slowed by Tradition

Thus, ancient Mesopotamian medicine, though primitive by modern standards, did provide some practical benefits and cures for various ailments. The problem was that doctors became caught up in accepted, time-honored traditions of religion and magic. This kept them from experimenting and advancing, as the Greeks later did. "In its two thousand or so years of existence," scholar Karen R. Nemet-Nejat points out, "Mesopotamian medicine made little progress. The doctors still resorted to superstition and magical explanations. Though they could offer rational explanations for many symptoms and diseases, they never tried to collect data and theorize."[21] As a result, it would be more accurate to call Mesopotamian medicine a collection of folk beliefs and practices, or a social institution, than a true science.

 Chapter Three

ARCHITECTURE AND BUILDING METHODS

Of the several examples of technology developed and used by the inhabitants of ancient Mesopotamia, architecture and building methods were among the most visible and important. For the most part, domestic architecture and structures, including private houses, were unremarkable. It was the region's monumental, or large-scale, architecture—temples, palaces, and so forth—that used what was then state-of-the-art technology.

The buildings created with that technology were often enormous, ingeniously conceived, and beautiful. But the region has few natural deposits of stone suitable for monumental construction. So the materials used were more often than not impermanent, especially mud bricks, which deteriorate rapidly. Thus, as Stephen Bertman points out:

In all of Iraq, there is not a single ancient monument still standing intact that dates to Sumerian, Babylonian, or Assyrian times. Unlike the Egyptologist, who gazes at the pyramids of Gizah and the columned splendor of [the temple of] Karnak, the student of Mesopotamia must sadly contemplate foundations in the dust.[22]

City Planning

The monumental architecture produced by the Sumerians, Babylonians, and other Mesopotamians was primarily, by default, urban architecture. Large-scale structures such as towering defensive walls and battlements, palaces, temples, ziggurats, and so forth served the needs of cities. And they became hallmarks of the Sumerian cities that sprang into existence in southern Mesopotamia in the late fourth millennium B.C.

At first there was little in the way of conscious city planning. Streets, housing blocks, and town squares grew organically—that is, unevenly and as need dictated. Most streets were narrow and winding. In southern Mesopotamia, temples and other monumental structures were built near the centers of the cities; in northern Mesopotamia, by contrast, the bigger buildings more often clustered together in an "upper city," leaving private houses and shops in an adjoining "lower city."

Only later, when wealthy kings occasionally chose to rebuild an old city or build a new one from scratch, did cities in the region have formal plans. A notable example was the renovation of Nineveh by the Assyrian king Sennacherib (reigned ca. 704–681 B.C.). He decided to transform what had been a small, old, run-down town into a magnificent new capital. "I enlarged Nineveh," he brags in an inscription. "I widened its squares and made streets and avenues as light as day."[23] Apparently Sennacherib became swept away in this enormous

The remains of ancient Mesopotamian cities, like these ruins of a Sumerian city on the banks of the Euphrates River, give researchers information on their layout and architecture.

Sennacherib Rebuilds Nineveh

In an inscription that has survived, the Assyrian Sennacherib describes how he transformed the run-down town of Nineveh into a splendid new capital city:

I, Sennacherib, king of Assyria, conceived of the plan [for the new city] in accordance to divine inspiration and occupied my mind. I deported [various peoples] who had not bowed to my yoke [control], and I imposed [mass labor] on them and they made the bricks. . . . A park [I created] next to my palace. [In] order to make the fields [surrounding the city] flourish, I tore open mountain and valley with iron picks to dig a canal.

Quoted in Gwendolyn Leick, *Mesopotamia: The Invention of the City.* New York: Penguin, 2001, pp. 227–28.

task and showed a genuine talent for the work, including many technical aspects. In Gwendolyn Leick's words, he had a

considerable understanding of urban planning [in] an almost modern manner. For [much] of his reign, he concentrated on this enormous project. . . . Of particular interest were his hydraulic engineering works, which [supplied] water to the numerous parks and orchards that were [his] particular delight. Some of these well-constructed tunnels, dams, and aqueducts are still in use today.[24]

Materials and Methods

The materials that Sennacherib and other builders used included mud bricks made from clay, various kinds of wood and stone, and some metals, including gold, for decoration. Because the region had few forests and little native stone, wood and stone had to be imported, making them expensive. In comparison, clay was quite abundant in Mesopotamia. So most of the monumental structures erected in the cities were made of sundried or fired clay bricks. It was common to mix binding materials such as straw or sand with the clay to add extra strength. (Still, the bricks disintegrated quickly, necessitating frequent repairs. Many centuries later, when these buildings and the cities around them were abandoned, the ruined bricks crumbled, forming big mounds that today are called "tells.")

Workers also customarily used some kind of mortar to help keep the bricks in place. One type of mortar was made by mixing moist mud with powdered lime. Builders also used bitumen, a tarlike, petroleum-based substance, for mortar. They obtained the sticky bitumen from deposits that formed at ground level in a number of places, not realizing that vast stores of petroleum, which modern Iraqis now exploit, lay under their feet. Most bricks, as well as stone blocks when they were available, were simply stacked, one on top of another.

For the tops of doorways and passageways, two early technological advances—the post and lintel and the arch—were used. Bertman explains:

A horizontal beam (the lintel) was supported atop two vertical posts.

A reconstruction of the magnificent Ishtar Gate, originally built by Babylonia's King Nebuchadnezzar in the sixth century B.C., is an example of the use of the arch as an architectural device in ancient Mesopotamia.

The opening, however, could be made only as wide as the longest available beam. [Also, if] too much weight was placed on top of the lintel, the stress imposed could cause the lintel to crack and the structure to collapse. [The] engineering solution proved to be the arch, a Sumerian invention of the fourth millennium B.C. . . . Its secret was to transfer the weight outward and then downward into the ground, rather than bearing it solely upon itself. By building a series of such arches back to back, engineers were able to construct vaults that served as tunnels [or passageways].[25]

The first arches used in Mesopotamia were corbelled. "Corbelling," according to noted scholar L. Sprague de Camp, "is laying courses or layers of stone or brick so that each course overhangs the one below. When walls are corbelled out from two sides until they meet, a corbelled arch or vault results."[26] Later, the true arch, featuring a curved arc of wedge-shaped blocks meeting at a central keystone, became a common architectural device in the region.

When possible, the doors that stood beneath the lintels and arches, along with door and window frames and roofs, were made of wood. The least expensive kind of wood was from the date palm, which was native to Mesopotamia. But many of the larger structures used sturdier and more expensive cedar and other hardwoods imported from Syria, Palestine, or Armenia.

Building Temples

These elements—stacked mud bricks (with minimal use of stone), timber roofs and door frames, the post and lintel, and the arch—along with decorated support columns (pillars), remained basic to Mesopotamian monumental construction for thousands of years. Other design elements became common in certain types of buildings. Religious temples, for example, also featured altars and large statues (cult images) of the gods to which these structures were dedicated.

The influential design for the majority of Mesopotamian temples can be seen at the site of the ancient Sumerian city of Eridu, in what is now southeastern Iraq, near the Persian Gulf. A temple built there in the fourth millennium B.C. became a model for many later Sumerian, Babylonian, and other temples in the region. In its heyday, it had a spacious central hall with rooms running off of each side (similar to the nave and anterooms in a modern Christian church). The hall and side rooms rested on a raised terrace that people accessed by a brick staircase. Some of the platforms supporting other later temples towered to 40 feet (12m) or more, making them landmarks that could be seen for long distances.

New temples often incorporated parts of earlier temples on the same spot. This demonstrates the desire to maintain tradition and continuity with the past, a common characteristic of ancient Mesopotamian cultures. According to Leick:

Ashurnasirpal Builds a New Palace

Several Assyrian kings built imposing palaces. One of the greatest of these builders was Ashurnasirpal II (reigned ca. 883–859 B.C.). In the following inscription, he brags about building and decorating a new palace in the city of Nimrud:

That city had fallen into ruins. . . . I built [it] anew, and the peoples whom my hand had conquered, from the lands which I brought under my sway, [I] took and I settled them therein. . . . A palace of cedar, cypress, juniper, boxwood, mulberry, pistachio-wood, and tamarisk, for my royal dwelling and for my lordly pleasure for all time I founded therein. Beasts of the mountains and of the seas of white limestone and alabaster I fashioned, and set them up in its gates, I adorned it, I made it glorious, and put copper clothes-hooks all around it. Door-leaves of cedar, cypress, juniper, and mulberry I hung in the gates thereof; and silver, gold, lead, copper, and iron, the spoil of my hand from the lands which I had brought under my sway, in great quantities I took and placed therein.

Quoted in Daniel D. Luckenbill, ed., *Ancient Records of Assyria and Babylonia*, vol. 1. New York: Greenwood, 1989, p. 173.

A colossal statue of a winged human-headed bull was one of the many amazing features of the palace built by King Ashurnasirpal II in the ninth century B.C.

The idea of sealing the remains of earlier structures and their contents (to preserve their sanctity?) and then erecting the new building on top of the leveled ruins [was significant].

Thus, most Mesopotamian temples enshrined the substance of older temples and the very platform they stood on was made venerable [honored] by the accumulated sacred debris. As such, they became a visible sign of continuity and antiquity [great age].[27]

Lifting the timbers, bricks, stones, statues, and other components of temples (and other large structures) into place was long done almost entirely by hand. Large numbers of laborers, often aided by animals, hoisted them up or pulled them with ropes. In the first millennium B.C., a simple but effective crane was introduced by the Greeks and came to be used widely in Mesopotamia. Such a crane, de Camp explains, consisted "of one or more poles fastened together at the top and a block and tackle with pulleys." Workers pulled the rope "by means of a capstan [winch] or treadwheel (a large drum-shaped wheel [in which] men walked up the curving inner side to make the wheel turn)."[28]

Palaces and Ziggurats

Like temples, palaces were frequently built atop raised platforms and featured massive walls, high ceilings, many support columns, and large-scale statues. One of the finest early royal homes in Mesopotamia was that of Mari's King Zimri-Lim, built in the 1700s B.C. Archaeological evidence shows that it had more than three hundred rooms. Among the more notable later palaces in the region were those built by the Assyrian kings Sargon II, Ashurbanipal, and Sennacherib.

Of these, Sennacherib's so-called Palace Without Rival at Nineveh was particularly impressive. It had more than eighty rooms, some of them immense, and featured several pairs of huge man-headed bulls carved from stone, which guarded the entrances; lengthy, highly elaborate panels of carved reliefs showing battles and hunting scenes; and numerous tall columns made of cedar imported from Syria. Sennacherib himself boasted:

The former palace I greatly enlarged. I finished it and splendidly adorned it; to the amazement of all peoples I filled it with costly equipment. Beams of cedar [I] stretched across the roofs. Great door-leaves of cypress, whose odor is pleasant as they are opened and closed, I bound with a band of shining copper and set them up in their doors.[29]

Even bigger than a temple and a palace was the ziggurat, a striking monumental architectural form peculiar to ancient Mesopotamia. Ziggurats were immense pyramid-like buildings found mainly in cities. Most often they were located near temples, and like temples they were used for religious purposes.

Although the Mesopotamian ziggurats looked somewhat like Egyptian pyramids, the two forms were very different. Whereas Egyptian pyramids were built as tombs for monarchs or other royalty, ziggurats were intended as dwelling places of gods and places for religious worship. Also, ziggurats were solid structures lacking the chambers and passageways

The ziggurat that stands at the site of the ancient Sumerian city of Ur is the most famous structure of its type. Although it has been partially reconstructed, it was originally built at the end of the third millennium B.C.

that exist inside Egypt's large pyramids. Finally, Egyptian pyramids had no stairways on the outside. By comparison, ziggurats had large stairways or ramps that priests used to access small chapels or temples resting at the summit.

Ziggurats were built of enormous numbers of small clay bricks. Sumerian and Babylonian ziggurats were freestanding and separate from other buildings in a temple complex; in contrast, Assyrian ziggurats were most often attached directly to ground-level temples. These

giant structures were meant to be "stairways to heaven," by which priests (and sometimes kings) ascended upward to commune with divine forces. There was also a political dimension to ziggurats; they reflected the wealth, power, and prestige of the city-states or empires that could afford to build them.

Bridges and Water Movers

Although ancient Mesopotamian construction technology was applied mainly

Ziggurats Old and New

Ziggurats were the largest structures erected by ancient Mesopotamian builders. To date, excavators have found the remains of thirty-two ziggurats in and around the Mesopotamian plains. Four of these are in southern Iran, and most of the others are in Iraq. Particularly well preserved is the ziggurat at Choqa Zanbil (or Dur-Untash), near Susa, in southwestern Iran. More famous, however, is the one at Ur (in southeastern Mesopotamia), which is also largely intact. Unfortunately, only some sections of the base of the greatest ziggurat of all have survived. This immense edifice, the Etemenanki, located in Babylon, was dedicated to the chief Babylonian god, Marduk. In its prime, the Etemenanki featured three large staircases, which led to an upper temple. The form of the ancient ziggurat is so striking that some modern archi-

The design of the Hodges Library on the campus of the University of Tennessee is modeled after ziggurats found in ancient Mesopotamia.

tects have copied it for their own buildings. One of the better-known examples is the University of Tennessee's Hodges Library in Knoxville, which opened in 1987. Its large, stepped levels are modeled on ancient Mesopotamian versions.

---

to large-scale buildings in cities, it was occasionally put to use in the countryside. The most visible example was bridges. The Sumerians, Babylonians, Assyrians, and Persians built few big bridges, partly because of the local scarcity of stone and timber. Another factor was the tendency of the Tigris, Euphrates, and other rivers to shift their courses now and then. This made any large, permanent bridges obsolete. To get across rivers, therefore, people commonly used rafts and small

boats. (From time to time, soldiers on campaign built pontoon bridges, consisting of rows of boats placed side by side with wooden planks laid across their decks.)

The few large, permanent bridges that were built in the region were impressive, however. One was constructed by the Babylonian king Nabopolassar in about 600 B.C. Spanning the Euphrates, it was the world's earliest known large-scale bridge. The Greek historian Herodotus saw it when he visited Babylon in the fifth century B.C. and later wrote:

[The builder] ordered long stone blocks to be cut, and when they were ready [he] diverted the river into [a pre-dug] basin. And while [the] original bed of the stream was drying up, [he erected] an embankment on each side of the water's edge . . . then built a bridge over the river with the blocks of stone which had been prepared, using iron and lead [clamps] to bind the blocks together. Between the piers [vertical supports] of the bridge, squared lengths of timber [were] laid down for the inhabitants to cross by. [Finally] when [the] bridge [was] finished, the river was brought back into its original bed.[30]

Archaeologists have determined that the bridge was 380 feet (115m) long and rested on seven massive stone piers.

Another impressive Mesopotamian bridge was constructed by Assyria's King Sennacherib to carry the water channel of

An Egyptian man channels water from the Nile using a shaduf *similar to those invented in ancient Mesopotamia thousands of years ago.*

an aqueduct across a stream. Located at Jerwan, north of Nineveh, the bridge was some 90 feet (27m) long and 30 feet (9m) high. It rested on five stone arches made of blocks measuring 20 inches (51cm) on a side.

Another piece of technology associated with water in the region was a device designed to raise large amounts of the precious liquid from one level to another. When workers dug a canal running off of a river, they often installed a sluice gate on the riverbank to control the volume and flow of the water into the canal. This approach worked all right when the river's water level was normal. When the water level dropped below that of the gate, however, the flow of water into the canal stopped.

The solution to this problem was the invention of a water mover that later became known as a *shaduf* (an Arab term). It was a long pole with a bucket attached to one end and a counterweight attached to the other. The center of the pole rested on a fulcrum (a rock or block of wood). One or more people swiveled the pole on the fulcrum so that the bucket dipped into the river and filled. Next, they swung the device up and over the bank of the canal and emptied it into the canal. Herodotus witnessed the *shaduf* in action. "Artificial irrigation," he later wrote, "is used [in Mesopotamia], not, as in Egypt, by the natural flooding of the river, but by hand-worked [*shadufs*]. Like Egypt, the whole [of Mesopotamia] is intersected by [canals and] dykes."[31] The *shaduf* is still used by thousands of people across the Middle East and Africa (especially in Egypt). It represents still another example of something invented millennia ago in Mesopotamia and later given to the world.

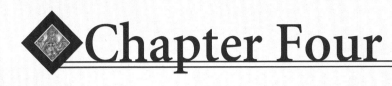

Chapter Four

AGRICULTURAL TOOLS AND EARLY WEAPONS

Tools and weapons were the earliest and most basic forms of technology produced by human beings. Simple stone tools and weapons were developed in Asia, Africa, and Europe tens of thousands of years ago in the Stone Age. But the pace of change and improvement for these implements was for a long time extremely slow.

Then, in the span of only a few centuries, the early peoples of the Near East, including Mesopotamia, introduced major improvements in traditional implements. They also invented new tools and weapons that became standard there and in other parts of the ancient world. These included vital farming tools, such as the plow and threshing sled; copper and later bronze tools and utensils, including knives, axes, chisels, nails, beakers, and brooches; and various kinds of swords and other weapons.

As the farming tools revolutionized agriculture in the Near East, so too did the weapons increase the efficiency, lethality, and scope of warfare in the region.

The First Farming Tools

The earliest important technological advances in Mesopotamia occurred in agriculture. People first began raising crops in about 9000 B.C. (or slightly earlier) in the Fertile Crescent, the fertile region stretching in a broad arc along Mesopotamia's western and northern rims. At first the farmers tilled the soil completely by hand, using sticks and sheer muscle power. Clearly, this was painstakingly slow and backbreaking work, so it was not long before specialized tools developed to make it easier. These tools were initially made of stone. The farmers used stone hoes to turn the earth, stone sickles to harvest the wheat, and heavy millstones to grind the grain.

When people from the Fertile Crescent began migrating onto the Mesopotamian plains between 6000 and 5000 B.C., they naturally brought their farming knowledge and tools with them. It was not long afterward—sometime in the 4000s B.C.—that the greatest technological advance yet took place. Some bright individual came up with the idea for a basic wooden plow. Modern scholars often call it a scratch plow; the ancient Mesopotamians called it an *ard.* In the words of A. Leo Oppenheim, for its time, "the Mesopotamian plow was a supreme technological achievement."[32] No longer was it necessary for farmers to rely solely on their own muscle power. By attaching the plow to oxen via ropes and leather harnesses, a farmer needed only to guide the plow while the beasts did most of the work. Obviously, this meant that a single farmer could grow and harvest more crops than he could before. And with the resulting increases in food supplies, the region could support larger local populations.

The next major agricultural advance occurred in the second millennium B.C. It was a more sophisticated version of the plow known as a seed plow (or a seeder plow or sowing plow). With the original

A sickle made from terra-cotta was one of the tools used by Sumerian farmers in the fourth millennium B.C.

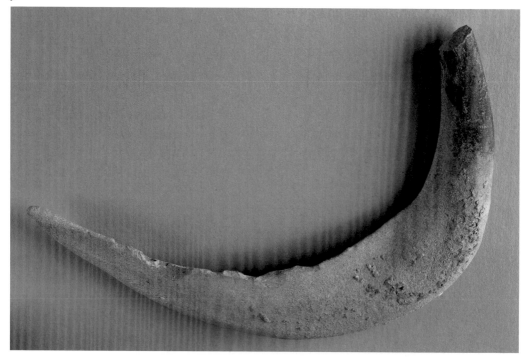

plow, after turning the earth the farmer (or his helpers) tossed the seeds by hand over the tilled field. But some of the seeds missed the furrows and were wasted. The seed plow overcame this drawback with a built-in, upright funnel that the farmer filled with seeds just prior to plowing. There was a small hole in the funnel's bottom. "When the seeds fell into the furrows cut by the plow," scholar Wolfram von Soden explains, "much less seed was lost on the ground . . . than was the case with hand-sowing."[33] It became part of local lore that the god Enlil, who oversaw and protected agriculture, had bestowed knowledge of the seed plow on humanity.

Another important agricultural tool developed by the early inhabitants of Mesopotamia was the threshing sled (or threshing board). Threshing, or separating the individual wheat grains from the stalks, had originally been accomplished by hand, which was a slow, tedious process. The threshing sled was designed to speed up this chore. It consisted of some wooden planks joined together to form a sled-like board about 4 to 6 feet (1.2 to 1.8m) long. Sharp rocks, and later metal blades, were attached to the bottom. When an ox or donkey pulled the device over piles of harvested wheat, the rocks or blades cut and mashed up the stalks, in the process separating out most of the grains.

Basic Metalworking Methods

The metal blades used in threshing sleds were almost always made of copper or bronze. In fact, these were long the two most resourceful metals used in Mesopotamia. People used them for utensils, weapons, figurines, jewelry, cookware, mirrors, and numerous other everyday things.

Copper was the first metal to be used for tools and weapons. The earliest human-made copper items discovered so far are a pin and bodkin (an awl-like instrument for making holes in fabric) dating from the period of 7500 to 7000 B.C. They were discovered in southeastern Anatolia (what is now Turkey), not far from Mesopotamia's northwestern border. Other early examples of copper items were found in Iran, Syria, and northern Mesopotamia. By the late 4000s B.C., copper was in wide use across the entire Near East.

Before people could use the copper to make tools and other items, they had to refine it. That is, they had to separate it from the ore (mixture of rock and metal) in which it is most often bound in its natural state. The refining process was often called "washing." The most common washing method was to heat the ore until the copper separated out and settled to the bottom of the furnace. At this point, the metal still contained various impurities. To remove them, metalsmiths used a process called smelting. "Smelting," H.W.F. Saggs explains, "means heating copper . . . with [small quantities of] charcoal to a temperature sufficient to [remove the impurities], leaving metallic copper. This reaction begins at temperatures of about 700 degrees C [1,484°F]."[34]

The Spread of Iron Technology

The techniques of making iron tools and weapons spread slowly but steadily through the Near East, including Mesopotamia, in the second millennium B.C. The late, noted scholar of Near Eastern civilizations, A. Leo Oppenheim, makes these general observations:

Although iron ore can be reduced at a lower temperature than copper ore, the product obtained could not be used in the same way as copper and bronze. It could not be cast. This had to be done at [a] high temperature, a technique first practiced by European metallurgists in the fourteenth century [A.D.]. On the other hand, iron, when hot, can be hammered into a desired form relatively easily. It can be changed into a kind of steel when repeatedly heated [and] quenched in cold water. [Over time, Mesopotamian metalsmiths perfected these techniques.] . . . With the coming of iron, there were certain dislocations in the trade routes that brought ores and metals to Mesopotamia and in the position of the smith of whom the working of iron demanded a much higher technical knowledge [than working with copper or bronze]. The desire to preserve the lore of their craft created secrecy [and] seclusion.

A. Leo Oppenheim, *Ancient Mesopotamia: Portrait of a Dead Civilization.* Chicago: University of Chicago Press, 1977, p. 322.

Once the copper was washed and purified, the smiths could use it to make whatever tools, weapons, or other objects they desired. One common approach was to pour liquid copper into premade stone or wooden molds of various shapes. When the metal dried, they removed the molds. They could also hammer the copper into the desired shape, a method routinely used in making swords, ax heads, and other bladed tools and weapons. The smiths had to be careful because of copper's unique qualities, as Saggs points out:

Repeated hammering gradually makes it [the copper] more brittle and eventually it refuses to respond to further hammering, except by cracking. If hammered copper is then heated, its malleability [pliable quality] is restored, making possible further modification of its shape by hammering.[35]

Early on, Mesopotamian smiths learned that mixing copper with other metals—producing alloys—made metal objects stronger and less likely to corrode. In particular, the use of bronze, an alloy of copper and tin, began during the middle to late fourth millennium B.C. and quickly became widespread in Mesopotamia. (Bronze-making also spread outward, reaching Greece, Egypt, and Iran in the centuries that followed.) Many of the same tools and weapons that had been routinely made from copper were now cast in bronze, making them sturdier and more reliable.

Finally, iron came into wide use in Mesopotamia in the early first millennium B.C. Refining and molding iron was more difficult, partly because it requires much higher temperatures. In fact, none of the furnaces used in ancient times could produce temperatures as high as iron's melting point, which is 1,538 degrees Celsius (2,800°F). So the smiths used a method called forging. They heated the iron until it turned into a spongy mass containing carbon and other impurities. Working the heated iron on a forge removed most of the impurities, producing wrought iron, which was pliable enough to shape into sword blades and other objects. The Assyrians became especially skilled at iron forging in the first millennium B.C. The swords and other weapons they made this way were a major factor in their success as empire builders.

The Introduction of Metal Weapons

Indeed, weapons-making technology was directly related to warfare methods and tactics; and as the technology improved, it stimulated changes in tactics. In turn, these changes made wars more lethal and perhaps more common. This cause-and-effect process occurred first in the landmark transition from stone to metal weapons. For millennia, people in Mesopotamia and other parts of the Near East had used stone maces (clubs), knives, axes, spearheads, and arrowheads in battle. Over time, these were replaced by metal versions. Soldiers and whole armies wielding metal weapons and armor were decidedly more fearsome than their Stone Age ancestors. This made possible the conquest of larger territories and populations.

One way that advances in metal weapons-making technology changed the nature of warfare was through an ongoing arms race. When one people or nation introduced a more effective offensive or defensive device, it always motivated one or more opposing peoples to invent a way to counter it. Metal helmets are a clear example. Before they were introduced, soldiers wore head guards made of layers of leather or felt. These offered only minimal protection against blows by maces and none at all against spear points or arrows. In contrast, metal helmets often deflected the blows of maces and even stone battle-axes (although the helmet did dent). In response, weapon makers developed a new kind of battle-ax. "Because of the increasing use of metal helmets," Edinburgh University scholar Trevor Watkins writes, "a new tactic was devised and a sharply pointed battleaxe began to appear."[36] If aimed skillfully, this weapon could pierce a copper or bronze helmet.

However, the adoption of metal weapons did not always result in major changes in warfare. Take, for example, the development of metal swords. The copper swords used in Mesopotamia and surrounding regions in the early fourth millennium B.C. could kill or maim a person if the user managed to strike a vulnerable spot on his opponent's body. But overall these swords had serious limitations. The main problem was that copper is a relatively soft metal. When a soldier swung a long copper blade in a hacking or slashing motion, there was an even greater chance the blade might break. At the least, it bent badly, rendering it largely ineffective.

For this reason, copper swords long remained backup weapons used in battle only when a soldier's spear or other primary weapon broke. Bronze swords were

The crushed skull of a soldier from the third millennium B.C. discovered in the Royal Cemetery of Ur bears a helmet made of copper, an example of how ancient Mesopotamians used weaponry crafted from various metals.

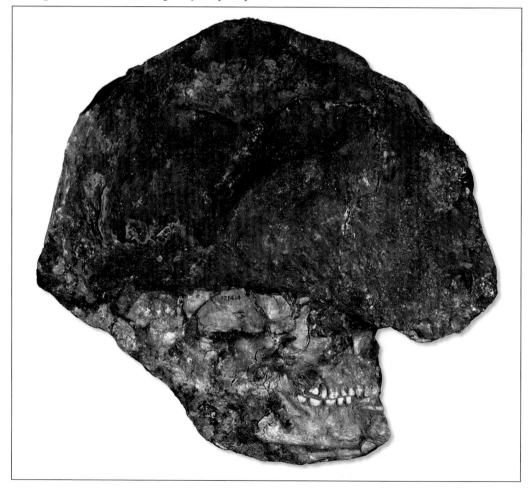

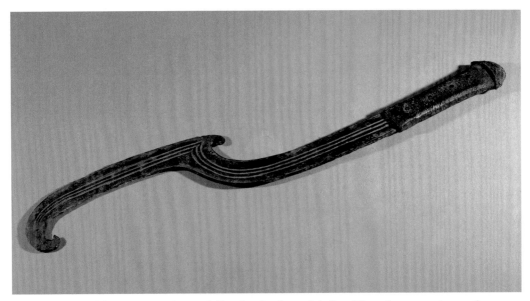

A dagger used by a Sumerian soldier in the late third millennium B.C. is made from copper or bronze. The use of copper and bronze to make weapons such as this eventually gave way in the first millennium B.C. to iron, which was more durable and less likely to fail in combat.

better, but not by much. It was not until much later—in the first millennium B.C., when iron blades came into wide use—that swords became reliable weapons in Mesopotamia. However, iron was more difficult, and therefore more expensive, to produce than bronze. Thus, not every soldier was equipped with an iron sword, and one-on-one sword fighting remained secondary to combat using other weapons.

Missile Weapons

For the most part, in fact, swords, maces, battle-axes, and daggers all ended up as secondary weapons in Mesopotamian warfare, mainly because close, hand-to-hand fighting was not the norm. Instead, weapons-making technology for infantry (foot soldiers) long centered on missile weapons, or those hurled at an enemy from a distance. One of the two chief kinds was the metal-tipped throwing spear, or javelin, which saw wide use among the Sumerian cities by the end of the fourth millennium B.C. It featured a long wooden staff with a sharpened blade of copper or bronze tied to the top by cords.

The other main missile weapon used in the region was the bow and arrow. At first the bow was the "self" or "simple" variety, made from a piece of wood measuring from 3.5 to 7 feet (1 to 2m) long. The bowstring was made of tightly twisted

The Basic Textile Tool

While the plow and threshing sled were basic tools of agriculture, the fundamental tool of the textile industry in ancient Mesopotamia was the loom. Regrettably, few depictions of looms from the region have survived. Most scholars think that the Sumerians, Babylonians, and other Mesopotamians used looms similar to those used in nearby Egypt, which are better documented. One was the simple ground loom. It consisted of a rectangular frame set horizontally on the ground or floor. The weavers stretched rows of thread (the warp) across the frame from top to bottom. Then they interwove other threads (the weft) at right angles into the warp. A somewhat more advanced loom probably came into use in the second millennium B.C. It also had a rectangular wooden frame. However, this time the frame was aligned in a vertical position and the weavers interwove the threads from the bottom up.

A relief from ancient Mesopotamia dated to the late fourth millennium B.C. depicts a weaver using a loom to make cloth.

The warp threads hung vertically from the top bar of the loom. These were weighted using small rocks or lumps of baked clay. The weaver sat in front of the loom and moved the odd-numbered warp threads backward and forward, intertwining them with the horizontal weft threads with the aid of a comb or stick.

animal gut. The arrows fired from such bows had copper or bronze tips.

With such missile weapons as their mainstay, military leaders adopted battlefield tactics in which many soldiers threw their javelins or shot their arrows in large-scale volleys at the enemy ranks. The idea was to kill or wound enough opponents early on to instill fear and convince them to run away. Of course, this approach was blunted to some degree by the development of shields and body armor that could repel many of the incoming javelins and arrows. When this happened, the opposing forces usually did not run away. One approach was to keep on firing arrows from a distance in hopes of wearing down the enemy. But if this did not work, the dreaded butchery of hand-to-hand fighting became necessary.

The Emergence of Heavy Infantry

The Sumerians, who organized the first armies in Mesopotamia, continued to try to think of ways to counter new developments in weapons-making technology. Metal helmets, metal battle-axes, javelins and arrows with metal tips, and shields made from wood and layers of animal hides were all important innovations, some invented to counter others. But it was not long before the armies of all the major Sumerian cities had all these devices. Was there a way to break this stalemate?

As it turned out, there was. At some point in the third millennium B.C., someone realized that one way to counter all

A scene from the Stele of the Vultures, dated to 2500 B.C., depicts infantry soldiers in formation using spears and shields to confront enemy combatants.

"I Polished My Weapons"

This excerpt from a surviving Near Eastern document describes a fight between two ancient warriors of the region. The bows, battle-axes, and javelins they use are typical of Sumerian and early Babylonian warfare.

A mighty man of Retenu [Syria] came, that he might challenge me in my own camp. He was a hero without peer, and he had [beaten all opponents in his land]. During the night I strung my bow and shot my arrows [in a practice session] and I polished my weapons. When day broke . . . he came to me as I was waiting. [He] took his shield and his battle ax and his armful of javelins. Now after I had let his weapons issue forth [without doing me any damage], he charged me and I shot him, my arrow sticking in his neck. He cried out and fell on his nose. I [finished him off] with his own battle ax and raised my cry of victory. . . . Then I carried off his goods and plundered his cattle.

Quoted in James B. Pritchard, ed., *Ancient Near Eastern Texts Relating to the Old Testament.* Princeton, NJ: Princeton University Press, 1992, p. 20.

of these military elements was to arm and arrange one's troops in a more effective way. This marked the birth of what military experts later came to call heavy infantry, yet another Mesopotamian innovation that came to be used worldwide. In this case, the term *heavy* refers to the large amount of armor and weapons carried by and protecting each soldier. These men wore not only metal helmets but also heavy leather cloaks studded with metal disks, which protected their torso and upper legs. They also wielded long spears and very large shields that stretched from shoulder to ankle.

Even more frightening was the way these highly armored troops acted together. In the late 1800s French excavators discovered one of the most significant of all Mesopotamian artifacts in the ruins of the Sumerian city of Lagash. Scholars call it the Stele of the Vultures and date it to the 2500s B.C. The stone sculpture clearly shows a tightly packed formation of Lagash's heavy infantrymen, who are marching over the bodies of their opponents from the rival city of Umma. As Watkins describes it:

> The sculptor has clearly carved massed ranks [lines] of helmeted spearmen behind a front rank of men bearing shields. . . . What is significant is the number of spears projecting between the shields. The artist emphasizes the solidarity of the formation, protected from chin to ankle by the almost interlocking shields.[37]

This battlefield formation, which foreshadowed the even more fearsome Greek formation of the first millennium B.C., represented the state-of-the-art military technology of its day. It was designed either to mow down or to scare off enemy forces. Yet as effective as it must have been, it was soon to be replaced by even more efficient and deadly military innovations—a new, incredibly effective bow and the horse-drawn chariot.

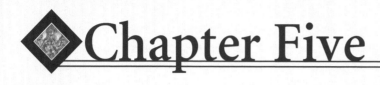

Chapter Five

ADVANCES IN WEAPONS TECHNOLOGY

In Mesopotamia, the third millennium B.C. had witnessed the spread of metal weapons, helmets, and armor; highly protective shields; and battlefield formations that effectively used these military tools. But as has been true throughout recorded history, some rulers and nations were not satisfied with the current state of things. They desired to conquer their neighbors. And if those neighbors had similar military power, that conquest would be long and difficult. Therefore, the search was always on for any new technological advances that might give ambitious individuals an edge in the relentless arms race.

One example consisted of periodic improvements in the quality of the metals used to make weapons and armor. When bronze first appeared, its quality was low. Though it was stronger and more durable than copper, it was still fairly bendable and there was much room for improvement. Better-quality bronze appeared in the second millennium B.C. and made traditional weapons, such as battle-axes, javelins, and daggers, along with helmets, more effective.

Ordinary straight swords were still inefficient for forceful hacking against shields and helmets. But new technological twists got around this problem to some degree by changing the shape of the blade. The most successful example was the *khopesh,* which came into wide use by about 1600 B.C. The blade was curved like that of a farmer's sickle. Instead of hacking with it in a downward stroke, a soldier used a horizontal slashing stroke. He aimed for his opponent's neck, wrist, calf, or some other unprotected spot and tried to inflict a serious injury.

Much more deadly and far-reaching in their effects were two new breakthroughs in military technology. One was the composite bow, which was initially used in warfare in the late third millennium B.C. The other was the war chariot. It came into its own after the introduction of certain key advances in woodworking in the second millennium B.C. The new bow allowed soldiers to wound or kill the enemy from a great distance, while the chariot gave elite warriors an unprecedented degree of speed and mobility on the battlefield.

The Deadly Composite Bow

The basic idea for the first of these innovations, the composite bow, did not originate in Mesopotamia. Early versions of it had existed centuries before in parts of central Asia. But some sort of technical breakthrough, the nature of which is still uncertain, took place in Mesopotamia that made the weapon powerful and practical enough to use in large-scale warfare.

The term *composite* indicates something made up of several components or parts; indeed, the bow featured four main materials—wood, animal horn or bone, animal sinew (tendon) or gut, and glue. Moreover, the wooden sections were usually composed of two, three, or four different kinds of wood, each having certain desired properties. Trevor

A relief from the ninth-century B.C. palace of King Ashurnasirpal II shows soldiers paired in combat, one holding a shield for protection while the other fires a bow.

Watkins speculates about its construction and operation:

To the originally curved wooden bow, it is necessary to glue gut on the outer side and long slivers of bone on the inner [side]. As the bow is drawn, the gut is stretched and the bone is compressed. The composite bow gives a higher velocity [speed] than the simple longbow, is much shorter (and therefore much easier to use, for example, in a chariot), and is capable of being kept strung for long periods without distortion or loss of power.[38]

That power was impressive. The composite bow could fire an arrow up to 400 yards (364m) or more. It must be emphasized, however, that shots taken at that distance were far from accurate. Even the most skilled bowmen could not achieve effective accuracy beyond 150 yards (137m). Nevertheless, the weapon could fire arrows faster and at higher speeds than conventional bows. A military leader could order hundreds of archers armed with the new bow to fire from a great distance. The resulting massed volley of arrows might cause confusion and fear among the enemy, perhaps enough to make them withdraw. More importantly, skilled archers standing closer (either on foot or in chariots) could do considerable damage to the enemy ranks. This was true even when the opponents were carrying

Making a Composite Bow

Noted military historian John Keegan offers this concise but detailed description of the construction of an ancient composite bow:

The composite bow began as five pieces of plain or laminated wood, [forming] a central grip, two arms and two tips. Once glued together [by glue made from boiled-down cattle tendons and skin mixed with fish skins], this timber "skeleton" was then steamed into a curve, opposite to that it would assume when strung. And steamed strips of [animal] horn were glued to the "belly" [inner side of the bow]. It was then bent into a complete circle, again against its strung shape, and [animal] tendons were glued to its "back" [outer side]. It was then left to "cure" [dry, which could take many months]. And only when all its elements had [stuck firmly together] was it untied and strung for the first time. Stringing a composite bow, against its natural relaxed shape, required both strength and dexterity.

John Keegan, *A History of Warfare.* New York: Random House, 1993, pp. 162–63.

shields since at close range arrows from a composite bow could pierce many standard shields.

To be sure, the new technology did have a few drawbacks. First and foremost, composite bows were specialty items with multiple parts. That made them quite expensive to make. Also, they required "long construction times of at least one year for a good bow," says University of Wales scholar Simon Anglim, "and ten [years] for a superb one. [In addition] they required much skill, strength, and practice,"[39] so training the archers was also an expensive task.

Just as spears and shields were more effective when used in strategic formations, composite bows were more deadly when used in certain ways. Firing them from charging chariots, for example, could be devastating for those who were under attack. For foot archers, the technology was used in a different way. A new tactical field unit built around these fighters developed in the second millennium B.C., reaching high levels of efficiency under the Assyrians. Called the archer pair, it consisted of two men. One held a large, body-length shield to deflect arrows and any other missiles sent by the enemy. The other man, armed with the composite bow, stood behind the shield and fired one arrow after another. Lines containing hundreds or even thousands of these archer pairs moved forward in unison during a battle, unleashing lethal volleys from their composite bows.

Early Battle Cars

As a piece of technology, the composite bow has sometimes been called a simple machine (a device with moving parts that accomplishes work). A more complex machine, one often used in conjunction with the composite bow, developed in ancient Mesopotamia and rapidly transformed warfare far and wide. This was the chariot. An expert on the device, historian Arthur Cotterell, has stated:

[The] most charismatic [compelling] war machine ever invented, the chariot altered the face of war throughout the ancient world. Its impact was dramatic, as thousands of chariots clashed in fast-moving encounters which [often] determined the outcome of battle.[40]

It is important to emphasize that the kind of chariots portrayed in movies such as *The Ten Commandments* and *Ben-Hur*—elegant, lightweight, spoke-wheeled vehicles racing along at high speeds—took a long time to develop. When the Sumerians introduced the first chariots in the third millennium B.C., they were heavy, clumsy, and slow. Modern scholars call them battle wagons, battle carts, or battle cars. They featured floors, sides, and wheels made of solid wood. And each was pulled by four donkeys or onagers (wild asses), beasts that were relatively small and slow. These early chariots were not very agile or maneuverable, so they could not

The Royal Standard of Ur, dated to the mid-third century B.C., depicts Sumerian warriors riding wheeled carts into battle.

be used offensively—that is, in direct charges on enemy lines. According to University of Calgary scholar Christon I. Archer, "A charge toward a massed enemy would have been difficult, not only because of the reluctance of the animals to move into or over obstacles, [but] also because the lack of a swivel front axle made for a wide and awkward turning circle."[41]

Depictions of such battle cars appear prominently in the Stele of the Vultures as well as another carved panel from the same era (ca. 2500 B.C.), the Royal Standard of Ur. As shown in the Royal Standard, the primitive chariot is more of what experts call a prestige vehicle than a major weapon system. Archer explains:

It seems likely that this Sumerian battle car ran along the front or sides of an enemy force while jav-

elins or spears were thrown. Additionally, the chariot would chase the retreating enemy or bring high-ranking officers to the battlefield, who would then dismount to fight. No doubt the battle car acted as a psychological weapon as well, especially if the enemy did not possess such a weapon.[42]

Sleek, Swift Killing Machines

As the evolution of military technology continued in the Near East, the clumsy battle wagons used by the Sumerians steadily gave way to sleek, swift killing machines that revolutionized warfare. This could not have happened without the introduction of two major innovations that swept through the region in the second millennium B.C. First, Mesopotamian artisans developed more advanced woodworking methods. These made it possible to discard the old solid wheels and construct spoked wheels as well as build much more lightweight, contoured chariot bodies.

The second innovation was the use of horses. These animals, which had been in short supply in the region before, now began to be bred on a wider scale and were harnessed to chariots. (The Kassite rulers of Babylonia led the way in horse breeding and training.) Horses not only had more strength and endurance than donkeys and onagers, but they also were faster.

Lighter, more maneuverable chariots and the stronger, faster beasts drawing them were a powerful combination. Squadrons of chariots could now be used for shock action—direct offensive attacks on infantry. Javelins and arrows launched from oncoming chariots wounded or killed foot soldiers or sent them into flight. Moreover, chariots could now be used for even more than frontal assaults, as Anglim points out:

A horse-drawn war chariot carrying several Assyrian soldiers with shields and bows is depicted in a ninth-century B.C. relief from the palace of King Ashurnasirpal II.

Improvements in Chariot Design

The introduction of lightweight chariots in the second millennium B.C. was an important watershed in ancient warfare. In the following millennium, the Persian king Cyrus II (reigned 559–530 B.C.) introduced further improvements in these wheeled vehicles. In his account of Cyrus's life, the fourth-century B.C. Greek historian Xenophon writes:

He had chariots of war constructed with strong wheels, so that they might not easily be broken, and with long axles; for anything broad is less likely to be overturned. The box for the driver he constructed out of strong timbers in the form of a turret; and this rose in height to the driver's elbows, so that they could manage the horses by reaching over the top of the box; and besides, he covered the drivers with mail [armor], all except their eyes. On both sides of the wheels, moreover, he attached to the axles steel scythes [blades] with the intention of hurling the chariots into the midst of the enemy.

Xenophon, *Cyropaedia*, vol. 1, trans. Walter Miller. New York: Macmillan, 1914, pp. 135–37.

[Fast-moving] chariot forces could pass around infantry formations to attack them in the flank [side] or rear. They also patrolled [barricades] during sieges, scouted, carried out raids, and skirmished [fought small battles] in advance of the main forces. Given these capabilities, it would have been difficult for any people [in the region] to maintain their independence without having chariots of their own. In effect, this meant every civilized state in the Near East required them [and] the only way to gain superiority was to build and maintain as many as possible.[43]

Seeking this sort of military superiority, in the thirteenth and twelfth centuries B.C. the Assyrians poured much time and money into further improvements in chariot technology. This expanded the capabilities of these vehicles, making the Assyrian army widely feared. "Changes in technology," military historian D.J. Wiseman writes, made possible the

design [of] a light vehicle with a wooden frame set on a metal undercarriage with the wheel axis moved back from the center to the rear. The result was a highly maneuverable vehicle which required less traction effort. . . . The chariot's driver was held steady against the front screen while the rigid shaft, originally elliptical [oval] but later straight, made control of the two yoked horses easier. The car became increasingly rectangular in shape to accommodate more armor and crew.[44]

In the centuries that followed, the Assyrians, Babylonians, Egyptians, and others continued to improve chariot technology and effectiveness. In addition to some minor technical changes, they expanded the size of the vehicle's crew. For a long time, it had remained at two, a driver and a warrior (except in Anatolia, where the Hittites utilized a third man early on). Starting in the eighth century B.C., the standard Assyrian chariot had a third man—a shield bearer charged with protecting the other two crewmen from incoming arrows and javelins. Another change was outfitting the onboard warrior in body armor. Sculptures and paintings from Egypt, Palestine, and other parts of the Near East during this period show suits of armor featuring copper or bronze scales sewn or glued to heavy leather or linen shirts.

A Famous Chariot Battle

The power and importance of chariot technology at its height is best illustrated by the way it was used on Near Eastern battlefields. The earliest battle in world history for which a detailed account has survived also happened to be one of the greatest chariot battles ever fought. It took place at Kadesh (or Qadesh) in Syria in 1275 B.C. The Hittites, from Anatolia, opposed the Egyptians under their new pharaoh (king), Ramesses II. (At the time, both the Hittites and Egyptians shared a fragile balance of power with the nearby Assyrians and other Mesopotamians.) The Hittites had about thirty-seven thousand infantry and twenty-five hundred chariots, compared to the Egyptians' eighteen thousand foot soldiers and perhaps two thousand chariots.

Shortly before the fight began, the Hittites tricked Ramesses into thinking they were camped many miles away. In truth, the Hittite soldiers and chariots were hiding on the far side of Kadesh, preparing to ambush the Egyptians. By the time the Egyptian king found out, it was too late to warn one contingent of his army, which was nearing the Orontes River, a few miles south of the city. A huge mass of Hittite chariots suddenly appeared and charged right at the unprepared Egyptians. Many were killed, and the rest ran for their lives to Ramesses' camp.

There, the pharaoh mustered his own troops and chariots and hurried to counterattack the oncoming Hittite chariots. In an incredible display of driving skill and sheer firepower, Ramesses and his men turned the tide of battle. The Egyptian chariots attacked the enemy's

A relief from the temple of
Egyptian king Ramesses II
depicts the use of chariots
as his forces clashed with
the Hittites at the Battle
of Kadesh in 1275 B.C.

The Chariots at Karkar

One of the largest chariot battles in which ancient Mesopotamians took part was that fought at Karkar (or Qarqar) in Syria in 853 B.C. The army of Assyria's King Shalmaneser III faced off with a coalition of smaller armies from various Syrian and Palestinian kingdoms. The number of Assyrian chariots is uncertain. But one of Shalmaneser's inscriptions does break down the opposing forces, which had 3,940 chariots in all.

[King] Hadadezer [of Damascus]: 1,200 chariots, 1,200 horsemen, 10,000 foot soldiers; [King] Irhuleni of Hamath: 700 chariots, 700 horsemen, 10,000 foot soldiers; [King] Ahab the Israelite: 2,000 chariots, 10,000 foot soldiers; . . . [the king of] Arqad: 10 chariots, 10,000 foot soldiers; . . . [the king of] Shian: 30 chariots, 10,000 foot soldiers.

Quoted in Arthur Cotterell, *Chariot: The Astounding Rise and Fall of the World's First War Machine.* New York: Overlook, 2005, p. 236.

vehicles from the side and rear. Then a large group of Egyptian reinforcements arrived. And they, too, charged the Hittites. According to scholar Mark Healy:

> The Hittite force visibly wavered, then began to retreat, [while] Rameses and elements of his chariotry [closed in from the south]. In a running battle all the way back to the river, the Egyptians poured [volleys of arrows] from their composite bows into the now rapidly depleting Hittite ranks. . . . Desperate to save their lives, the leading [Hittite] charioteers plunged into the Orontes in a fatalistic bid to escape the rapidly closing Egyptians.[45]

The Decline of the Chariot

At the time of the showdown at Kadesh, and for several centuries afterward, chariot technology and the firepower it produced ruled most of the large battlefields of the Near East. But this state of affairs was not destined to last. Just as people had learned to counter military technologies in the past, they eventually made chariots out of date as well. By the time of the rise of the Persian Empire (in the sixth century B.C.), chariots were already taking a secondary role in battle. One reason was the increasing use of cavalry—soldiers mounted on horses. Horsemen could throw javelins and shoot arrows, just as chariot warriors could. Moreover, cavalry was more flexible because individual horsemen could move over rough terrain in which chariots could not maneuver.

Another reason for the decline of chariots was that the Persians were the first Mesopotamians to fight wars against the Greeks. Greek foot soldiers were extremely well protected by armor. They were also trained to stop chariot charges. The Persian king Darius III tried using chariots against Alexander the Great when he invaded Mesopotamia in the 330s B.C. On cue, the Greek infantrymen stepped aside and allowed the oncoming vehicles to pass by; then they swarmed around the chariots and used javelins and spears to kill their crews.

The age of the war chariot was over. But other forms of military technology were still very much in play, including the naval variety. As it turned out, some of the greatest battles fought between the Persians and Greeks were on the water.

Chapter Six

SHIPS AND NAVAL TECHNOLOGY

The ships and ship-related technologies used by the ancient Mesopotamians can be conveniently divided into two broad categories. The first consisted of small boats used mainly for transporting people and supplies on rivers and in coastal waters. The second involved larger, more seaworthy warships to carry troops and engage fleets of enemy vessels.

It might be surprising to some that the Mesopotamians needed large numbers of boats. After all, with the exception of the shores of the Persian Gulf in the southeast, the region has no seacoasts. Indeed, it is true that, compared to the Greeks, Phoenicians, and some other Mediterranean peoples, the Sumerians, Babylonians, and Assyrians were veritable landlubbers. However, though these ancient Mesopotamians were not expert mariners, they did build and use large numbers of boats. They needed them because the flat (and sometimes rolling) plains they inhabited had numerous rivers, irrigation canals, and marshes. (The marshes were mainly in the south, along the big river deltas.) People regularly used these waterways for travel, transporting goods, and fishing.

As for naval warfare, little of any importance took place within Mesopotamia itself. So the Sumerians, Babylonians, and Assyrians did not construct fleets of warships of their own. Yet two later empires centered in Mesopotamia, the Persian and Seleucid realms, sometimes engaged enemies in naval battles in the Mediterranean region. So the Persians and Seleucids did maintain war fleets, though they tended to utilize ships maintained by subject peoples who lived on the seacoasts. The large naval battles fought by these Mesopotamian powers were few in number, but their consequences were at times far-reaching. The Persians' loss to the Greeks in the Battle of Salamis in 480 B.C. is a clear example. Had the Persian vessels won the day, the Persians might have gone on to conquer much or all of Europe.

Diverse River Vessels

Before some of Persia's rulers began having plans for faraway Europe, most Mesopotamians were concerned mainly with their own neighborhood in the center of the Near East. Traveling through the Tigris-Euphrates valley by land was time-consuming. So whenever possible people used small boats to travel along the rivers (and, to a lesser degree, the irrigation canals).

To navigate these local waterways, people used both sailboats and rowboats. Because they were made of perishable materials such as wood and bundled reeds, none of the early ones has survived. However, archaeologists have found ancient models of these vessels in tombs, as Stephen Bertman points out:

From a grave at Eridu, dug before 4000 B.C., comes the baked clay model of a broad-bottomed sailboat, complete with a socket for a mast; holes . . . to tie the rigging; and a seat for the sailor to sit on. From a third millennium B.C. royal tomb at Ur comes a sleek rowboat crafted from silver, with seven rowing benches and oars.[46]

Along the region's larger rivers, people used full-scale versions of these boats as ferries for both travelers and supplies. Some of the vessels moved on their own power, of course, using either their sails or oars. But many others were pulled by ropes. In such a case, one end of the rope was tied to the front of the boat; two or more individuals on the riverbank held the other end and dragged the craft along.

From the standpoint of design and basic technology, the vessels in question came in diverse shapes, sizes, and materials. One common one, the coracle, or "turnip," was essentially a round reed basket that was calked, or sealed and waterproofed, on the bottom with a coating of bitumen (tar). Some of the laws issued by Babylonia's King Hammurabi in the early second millennium B.C. provided for proper caulking for boats, for instance:

If a shipbuilder builds a boat for someone, and does not make it tight [i.e., properly caulked], if during that same year that boat is sent away and suffers injury, the shipbuilder shall take the boat apart and put it together tight at his own expense. The tight boat he shall give to the boat owner.[47]

Another kind of reed boat was common in the marshy areas of southern Mesopotamia. It was a long, narrow canoe fashioned and used by poor hunters and fishermen. (They used the same technique

Phoenician Ships Rule the Sea

The Old Testament's book of Ezekiel contains the following description of Phoenician ships, which long dominated Mediterranean sea lanes. In using the pronouns you *and* your, *Ezekiel addresses himself to the Phoenician city of Tyre, which he predicts will be destroyed.*

The inhabitants of [the Phoenician cities of] Sidon and Arvad were your rowers. . . . The elders of Gebal and its artisans were within you, caulking your seams; all the ships of the sea with their mariners were within you, to barter for your wares. [Your] mighty warriors; they hung shield and helmet in you; they gave you splendor. . . . Tarshish [Spain] did business with you out of the abundance of your great wealth; silver, iron, tin, and lead they exchanged for your wares. Javan [Greece], [and] Tubal [in Anatolia] traded with you. . . . So you were filled and heavily laden in the heart of the seas. Your rowers have brought you into the high seas. [Your] riches, your wares, your merchandise, your mariners and your pilots, your caulkers, your dealers in merchandise, and all your warriors within you shall fall into the midst of the seas. [At] the sound of the cry of your pilots [ship captains] the countryside shakes, and down from their ships come all that handle the oar.

Ezekiel 27:8–29.

of bundling tough river reeds for building the walls of their humble homes.)

Still another river vessel common to ancient Mesopotamia was the *kelek*, a small craft featuring a wooden frame with animal hides stretched over it. They were also sometimes made of inflatable goatskins, which helped them to float. The Greek historian Herodotus saw *keleks* in action when he visited Babylonia in the fifth century B.C. "The thing which surprised me the most of all in this country," he later wrote,

were the boats which ply down the Euphrates to the city. These boats are circular in shape and made of [animal] hides. They build them in Armenia, to the northward of Assyria, where they cut tree branches to make the frames and then stretch skins taut on the underside for the body of the craft. . . . The men fill them with straw, put the cargo on board—mostly wine in palm-wood casks—and let the current take them downstream. They are controlled by two men. Each has a paddle which he works standing up, one in front drawing his paddle towards him, the other behind, giving it a backward thrust.

Herodotus emphasized that *keleks* had the added benefit of being portable and in many ways recyclable. He told how most were dismantled after being used for one downstream trip and the hides were saved to make a new boat later upstream: "When they reach Babylon and the cargoes have been offered for sale, the boats are broken up, the frames and straw sold, and the hides loaded on donkeys' backs for the return journey overland to Armenia."[48]

Seagoing Vessels

Mesopotamians, particularly merchants and fishermen, also plied the waters of the Persian Gulf and on occasion the Indian Ocean beyond the gulf. For these ventures, they required craft larger and stronger than ones designed for river travel. The exact designs and technical aspects of these seagoing vessels are uncertain. Evidence suggests that they were powered by sails and that some had rudders for steering while others used one big oar to steer. When appropriate, these and other larger Mesopotamian boats were lashed together and connected by wooden planks to make artificial pontoon bridges across bays and channels.

These seagoing Mesopotamian ships may have been similar to, though perhaps

A relief dated to 700 B.C. from the palace of King Sennacherib depicts a Phoenician warship. The Phoenicians were also known for their merchant ships, which enabled them to create an extensive trade network in the Mediterranean.

Eyewitness to a Sea Battle

An eyewitness account of the Battle of Salamis, fought between the Greeks and Persians in 480 B.C., has survived. It appears in The Persians, *written by the Athenian playwright Aeschylus, who fought in the battle. In the play, he has a Persian messenger return to Mesopotamia and tell the king's mother:*

A Greek ship charged first, and chopped off the whole stern of a Persian galley. Then charge followed charge on every side. At first by its huge impetus our fleet withstood them. But soon, in that narrow space, our ships were jammed in hundreds; none could help another. They rammed each other with their prows of bronze; and some were stripped of every oar. Meanwhile the enemy came round us in a ring and charged. Our vessels heeled over; the sea was hidden, carpeted with wrecks and dead men; all the shores and reefs were full of dead. Then every ship we had broke rank and rowed for life. The Greeks seized fragments of wrecks and broken oars and hacked and stabbed at our men swimming in the sea. . . . The whole sea was one din of shrieks and dying groans, till night and darkness hid the scene.

A bust depicts the Greek playwright Aeschylus, who fought in the Battle of Salamis in 480 B.C. and wrote about his experience in a work titled The Persians, *thus providing historians with a detailed account of the events of the day.*

Aeschylus, The Persians, in *Aeschylus: Prometheus Bound, The Suppliants, Seven Against Thebes, The Persians,* trans. Philip Vellacott. Baltimore: Penguin, 1961, p. 133.

somewhat smaller than, the sail-driven merchant vessels used by Mediterranean peoples known for their maritime prowess. Some of these peoples, notably the Phoenicians of Syria-Palestine and the Greeks who lived in western Anatolia, eventually became subjects of Mesopotamian rulers. And these rulers took full advantage of existing ships in the area, especially Phoenician ones.

Like the Greeks, the Phoenicians had warships, which were generally long, narrow, and mainly propelled by rows of oarsmen. But the Phoenicians were more famous for their merchant vessels, which sailed to every Mediterranean coast. These ships were from 40 to 80 feet (12 to 24m) or more long, built wide and tall to create spacious interiors for holding bigger cargoes, and outfitted with a large square sail attached to a central mast.

Such merchant vessels became part of a successful trade route and network that Mesopotamian traders and rulers, beginning with the Assyrians and Persians, tapped into. It began in faraway India and Arabia, passed through the Persian Gulf and Babylonia, and connected with the Mediterranean region via Phoenician vessels and their fearless captains. Noted historian Lionel Casson explains:

> For centuries the inhabitants of the northern end of the Persian Gulf had been trading with India and [southern] Arabia. [The] products involved were for the most part luxuries: ivory, silks, and spices from India [and] incense and perfumes from Arabia. . . . What arrived at the Persian Gulf was transported [through Mesopotamia] by caravan to the Phoenician ports, especially Tyre.[49]

A Need for Warships

When they saw fit, Mesopotamian rulers also used Phoenician warships in various ways. A well-known example occurred in the 690s B.C., when Sennacherib (who expanded Nineveh into a major city) was king of Assyria. At the time, the Assyrians controlled Babylon and the rest of southern Mesopotamia. Suddenly, a Babylonian usurper, Merodach-Baladan, launched a rebellion in an attempt to drive the Assyrians out of that region. Sennacherib managed to chase the usurper away. But the Babylonian rebels kept up their resistance, making a home base in the extensive marshlands in the far south.

Sennacherib reasoned that sending warships into the marshes would help wipe out the rebels. So in a bold move he ordered his Phoenician subjects to build a special fleet of war galleys. The vessels were constructed in sections, which were carried overland to the Euphrates River. There, the ships were assembled. Then, well-trained crews sailed them down the river to the marshes, where the ships were instrumental in defeating the king's enemies.

Putting aside the significant technical achievement of assembling ships from ready-made sections far from a seaport, Sennacherib's use of warships in Babylonia was exceptional. Large Mesopotamian empires usually had no need for fleets of warships within the Tigris-Euphrates valley itself. But the Assyrian, Persian, and Seleucid realms held the lands along the eastern shores of the Mediterranean Sea. Thus, it was helpful to have fleets available in these waters to deal with rebellions or foreign threats in

Warriors travel by foot and over water in an Assyrian military campaign depicted in a relief from the palace of King Sennacherib, dated to 700 B.C.

that region. In such cases, it was easier and cheaper to use existing Phoenician or Greek ships than to try to organize an Assyrian or Persian warship-building industry from scratch.

The Persians used this approach to naval warfare more often and on a larg- er scale than the Assyrians did. This is partly because the Persian Empire was larger than the Assyrian one and had more subject peoples located on Medi- terranean shores. At various times dur- ing the sixth, fifth, and fourth centu- ries B.C., the Persians controlled Egypt,

Syria-Palestine (including Phoenicia), and the western and southern coasts of Anatolia. Most of these areas had rich seafaring traditions.

The Greek and Phoenician warships the Persians used were mostly triremes. A typical trireme of the fifth and fourth centuries measured from about 100 to 130 feet (30 to 40m) long, 15 to 18 feet (5 to 6m) wide, and carried a crew of about 200. Of these, 170 were oarsmen who sat in rows running along the sides of the vessel. The other men were sailors and fighters, including archers and warriors armed with spears and swords.

The main strategies of the crews of triremes were to sink or board and capture enemy ships. The most common tactic was to ram an opposing vessel. If one could maneuver one's ship properly, a metal-covered wooden ram, often called a "beak," mounted on the ship's prow (front) punctured the enemy's hull, causing it to take on water and sink. In the chief boarding technique, sailors hurled grappling hooks or ropes that locked the two ships together, after which fighters from one ship jumped onto the other vessel and fought hand to hand.

From Victory to Defeat

It was ships, crews, and tactics like these that Persian commanders used to put

A painting by nineteeth-century Spanish artist Rafael Monleon y Torres depicts a pair of Greek warships known as triremes, which were used in the mid-first millenium B.C.

Laws Regulating Boats and Sailors

The famous law code of the Babylonian king Hammurabi contains the following statutes concerning the responsibility of sailors to do what they are hired to do. The existence of such laws shows how important boats and their proper care and operation were in everyday life in Mesopotamia.

If a man rents his boat to a sailor, and the sailor is careless, and the boat is wrecked or goes aground, the sailor shall give the owner of the boat another boat as compensation. . . . If a man hires a sailor and his boat, and provides it with corn, clothing, oil and dates, and other things of the kind needed for fitting it: if the sailor is careless, the boat is wrecked, and its contents ruined, then the sailor shall compensate for the boat which was wrecked and all in it that he ruined. . . . If a sailor wrecks anyone's ship, but saves it, he shall pay the half of its value in money.

Quoted in Richard Hooker, ed., "Mesopotamia: The Code of Hammurabi," World Civilizations, Washington State University, 1996. www.wsu.edu/~dee/MESO/CODE.HTM.

down a rebellion that had begun in 499 B.C. in Persian-controlled Anatolia. Most of the Greek cities located along the peninsula's Aegean coast made a bid for freedom from the rule of Persia's King Darius I. The final, climactic showdown took place in 494 at Lade, near the Greek city of Miletus in southwestern Anatolia. According to ancient sources, the Persian fleet had about 600 triremes. A majority of the triremes were Phoenician-built, but there were also ships from Caria in southern Anatolia, the large Mediterranean island of Cyprus, and Egypt, all of which were then controlled by Persia. The opposing Greek war fleet had roughly 350 triremes.

Though they were outnumbered, the Greeks might have had a chance for victory if they had remained united. But they did not. Soon after the battle began, contingents from some of the Greek cities retreated. Among those who fled were the Samians from the island of Samos. According to Herodotus's account:

The sight of the Samians under sail for home was too much for the Lesbians [from the island of Lesbos], who were next in the line. They soon followed suit, as indeed did the majority of the Greek fleet. Of those who remained at their posts and fought it out . . . were the Chians [from the island of Chios], who fought a brilliant and most valiant action.[50]

A work by German artist Hermann Joseph Knackfuss depicts the epic Battle of Salamis in 480 B.C., at which the Greeks outwitted and defeated the larger Persian fleet by trapping it in the region's narrow straits.

On hearing of the Persian victory at Lade, Darius may have assumed that any future naval battles against the Greeks would have similar results. If so, it was a major miscalculation. When his son Xerxes launched a huge invasion of the Greek mainland fourteen years later, one of history's most pivotal naval battles took place in the Salamis straits southwest of Athens. Once more, the Persian fleet was larger than the Greek one. But this time the Greeks stayed united and fought with bravery and determination that has become legendary. According to Cornell University scholar Barry Strauss:

The narrow space [within the straits] made it impossible for the Persians to use their superiority in [numbers]. Their boats collided with each other. [This and other factors] turned the battle of Salamis from a hammer blow by Persia into a trap laid by Greeks. Persia hoped to crush the Greeks . . . but blundered into an ambush in which its [fleet's] very mass worked against it. Rarely have so many been hurt by so few.[51]

Later, the Mesopotamian-based Seleucid kings also used warships built by Greeks and other maritime peoples to fight for control of the eastern Mediterranean region. But like the Persians, they failed more often than they succeeded. In the end history proved, as it has many times since, that people fighting far from home and using technologies with which they have limited experience rarely win in the long run. By contrast, Assyrian and Persian armies were much more successful attacking cities inside Mesopotamia and neighboring regions; early on, well before most Europeans did, they became masters of siege technology.

Chapter Seven

FORTIFICATIONS AND SIEGE TECHNOLOGY

S ieges—the attack and capture of forts, walled cities, or other fortified places—were fairly common events in Mesopotamia and other sectors of the Near East in ancient times. It is uncertain when the first sieges took place, but from very early times, towns had outer walls and other defenses. Many modern scholars believe that the very existence of such fortifications indicates that attempts to capture or destroy these towns did occur. Indeed, "from the time that mankind began to settle in cities, the siege as a form of warfare was born," Simon Anglim says.

One of the primary purposes of the early development of cities was defense. [This is] illustrated by the large amount of early settlements upon naturally defensible terrain, such as hilltops, and the appearance of walled cities very shortly after the major urban centers were founded in the Near East. [As] these proved so easily defensible, any imperialist [militarily aggressive] state that sought a firm and lasting grip on an empire had to discover a way of reducing the advantage possessed by these urban fortresses.[52]

Among these large, militarily ambitious states, the Assyrian Empire was the first in history to use siege technology on a large scale. Assyrian military planners either invented or perfected older versions of nearly all the siege devices and techniques used later in Mesopotamia, other parts of the Near East, and Europe.

Early Fortified Towns

Of the older fortifications and siege technology the Assyrians inherited, some likely went back many thousands of years. In fact, even before towns appeared on the Mesopotamian plains, some settlements in the nearby Fertile Crescent featured defensive stone walls and towers. A few were quite impressive, notably some built in Palestine. Today the most famous example is Jericho (eventually a Hebrew town captured by the Assyrians). Situated not far north of the Dead Sea, it was among the more important early farming communities in the Fertile Crescent. (The locals grew barley, emmer wheat, and lentils.)

The ruins of the ancient city of Jericho include the remains of a defensive wall built to protect its inhabitants from siege. Parts of the wall are dated to 8000 or 7000 B.C.

Archaeological evidence shows that sometime in the ninth or eighth millennia (the 8000s or 7000s) B.C., Jericho's two to three thousand inhabitants surrounded their mud-brick houses with a stone defensive wall and a stone guard tower. The wall, the earliest of its kind yet discovered in the world, was about 13 feet (4m) high; the tower was about 26 feet (8m) tall and measured the same in thickness. Clearly, the residents would not have invested the time and effort needed to build such enormous battlements if they were not sometimes threatened with attack by their neighbors.

Much later, in the second millennium B.C., large defensive walls were still necessary at Jericho. The Old Testament's book of Joshua tells how the early Hebrews laid siege to Jericho and brought down its walls by shouting and blasting trumpets. (Historians assume this is an example of poetic license and that the attackers used more ordinary siege techniques.) After the city became part of the ancient kingdom of Israel, it remained fortified and strong until the Assyrians captured it in the eighth century B.C.

The Hebrews Besiege Jericho

One of the earliest recorded sieges in surviving ancient literature is the attack on Jericho by the Hebrews, who were then conquering Palestine. As written in the book of Joshua, the city falls as a result of religious rituals, aided by supernatural forces, rather than conventional siegecraft.

And it came to pass, when Joshua had spoken unto the people, that the seven priests bearing the seven trumpets of rams' horns passed on before the Lord, and blew with the trumpets [and] the armed men went before the priests that blew with the trumpets. . . . And the second day they compassed [circled around] the city once, and returned into the camp: so they did six days. And it came to pass on the seventh day, that they rose early about the dawning of the day, and compassed the city after the same manner seven times. [And] at the seventh time, when the priests blew with the trumpets, Joshua said unto the people, "Shout; for the Lord has given you the city. . . . So the people shouted when the priests blew with the trumpets [and] the wall fell down flat, so that the people went up into the city, every man straight before him, and they took the city. And they utterly destroyed all that was in the city, both man and woman, young and old, and ox, and sheep, and ass, with the edge of the sword.

Joshua 6:8–21.

Another important early fortified Near Eastern town was Çatal Hüyük (pronounced *chat-al hoo-YUK*) in southeastern Anatolia. It was established perhaps as early as 8000 B.C. but enjoyed its greatest prosperity in the seventh and sixth millennia B.C. In this period, Çatal Hüyük covered an area of about 32 acres (13ha), very large for a Stone Age town. Perhaps because its inhabitants owned large amounts of crops, animals, and other valuable commodities, bandits and/or neighboring towns attacked it from time to time. This seems certain because of the way the settlement was fortified. The "square, flat-roofed houses were built side by side like a pile of children's building blocks, pushed together," Trevor Watkins explains.

> Access to each house was by means of a door at roof-level, from which a steep ladder led down into the living area. Circulation [movement] around the settlement was across the flat roofs. The edge of such a settlement would have presented a solid, blank wall to any intruder or attacker. Once the ladders [were] drawn up, the settlement would have been impregnable [invincible, or secure].[53]

No one knows if Çatal Hüyük ever endured a long siege. Probably it did not, simply because it is unlikely that significant siege technology had developed yet. For historians, one question remains: When did the specialized devices and tactics for capturing fortified places first appear? For the moment, the best guess is that siegecraft (the techniques of siege warfare) developed a little at a time over many centuries in Mesopotamia and other parts of the Near East. It seems likely that the creation of cities with hefty defensive walls by the Sumerians (in the late fourth millennium B.C.) stimulated the invention of ways to breach those walls.

Siege Measures and Countermeasures

In whatever manner siegecraft developed in the region, it is certain that the Assyrians and Babylonians had a sophisticated knowledge of it and used it frequently during their conquests of neighboring lands. In fact, the Assyrians became masters of siege warfare. Two reasons for this may be that, first, their empire lasted a long time, and second, the Assyrian kings conducted military campaigns on an almost yearly basis. As a result, Assyrian armies had a great deal of experience in warfare as well as more need and opportunities to conduct sieges of enemy towns. This need motivated them to perfect older siege techniques and, when certain situations required it, to devise new ones.

Not surprisingly, city planners across the Near East responded to these advances in siegecraft by developing improved, more intimidating defenses. In turn, this stimulated the besiegers to invent still more ingenious methods of assault. As military historian Peter Connolly aptly

A siege machine is depicted during an assault on a fortification while defenders attack from above in a relief from the palace of King Ashurnasirpal II dated to the ninth century B.C.

puts it, "Fortification and siege warfare are inextricably combined [so connected that they cannot be separated]. The development of one inevitably stimulates changes in the other."[54]

A clear example of fortifications inspiring advances in siege technology, and vice versa, is the battering ram. In ancient times, it consisted of a large timber beam (sometimes with a metal tip) carried by men or dragged by animals. Its function was to knock down a city's front gate or crash a hole in a section of the defensive wall. Early on, city planners developed countermeasures to battering

rams. One was to dig a moat in front of the gate to make it harder for the ram to approach. Another countermeasure was to hurl rocks and boiling liquids down onto the men and animals operating the ram. In turn, the besiegers learned to counter these countermeasures. The Assyrians, for instance, covered a ram and the men moving it with a protective canopy made of wood, thatch, and/or layers of animal hides. As D.J. Wiseman points out, "Attempts by defenders to set fire to these [protected rams] by pouring burning oil or torches down on them usually failed, for the Assyrians devised contraptions to dowse the canopy with water."[55]

Over time many more measures and countermeasures developed in defenses and siegecraft in the Near East. For example, defenders made the lower sections of their outer walls extra thick to better withstand the attack of battering rams. In response, besiegers concentrated their efforts on the thinner, more vulnerable upper sections of the walls. To reach these heights, they used wooden scaling ladders. They also had large groups of bowmen shoot arrows at the defenders stationed at the top of the walls. To counter these attacks, the defenders used long poles to push the scaling ladders away from the walls. In addition, they protected themselves from incoming arrows by building square stone notches (merlons) separated by openings (crenels) atop the walls. They then hid behind the notches and fired their own arrows through the openings.

Sounds of the Siege

As noted scholar Barry Strauss puts it, the sounds created during a siege of an ancient Near Eastern walled city would have also been "an assault on the senses," a mix of

Forces led by King Ashurbanipal are depicted in a relief from his palace laying siege to an Egyptian city in 645 B.C., using all manner of the day's technology and weaponry.

visions and sounds that probably unsettled the participating soldiers and terrified any civilians present.

We might imagine the twanging of bowstrings, the hum of javelins in motions, the swish of slings, the bang of missiles [arrows and rocks] hitting shields that protected soldiers' backs as they climbed the scaling ladders, the crash of falling ladders, the thud of the battering ram against the doors of the gate, the grunts of the defenders as they tried to absorb the blow and hold the doors in place, the moans of the wounded, the crack of whip on horseflesh and the whinnying of the frightened beasts, [and] the blare of the trumpet ringing out the call to one last charge.

Barry Strauss, *The Trojan War*. New York: Simon and Schuster, 2006, p. 83.

Now it was the besiegers' turn to find new ways of countering these improved defenses. Perhaps the most successful was the siege tower. A tall wooden structure made of wood and thatch, it moved on large wooden wheels. Soldiers rode inside a tower and fired arrows into the city as they approached the walls. When the tower reached the walls, these troops climbed out and fought hand-to-hand combat with the defenders at the tops of the walls. One countermeasure against siege towers was to shoot burning arrows at them, hoping to set them ablaze.

Meanwhile, far below, other besiegers were digging tunnels (saps) under the walls. One aim was to give the attackers access to the city; another was to weaken a wall enough to make it collapse. To counter the saps, the defenders lit fires that filled the tunnels with smoke. They also dug their own tunnels beneath those of the besiegers, causing the upper saps to cave in.

Documented Assyrian and Persian Sieges

These and other examples of Mesopotamian fortifications and siege technology are plainly documented in ancient relief sculptures, especially those that adorned the Assyrian royal palaces. Among the most detailed and revealing are those of King Sennacherib. In 701 B.C. his forces besieged the Hebrew city of Lachish (in the Palestinian kingdom of Judah), an event described in the Old Testament's second book of the Chronicles.

Sennacherib's sculptors dutifully showed how the fortified town of Lachish was constructed atop a high, steep

Sennacherib Invades Judah

Sennacherib's sieges of Lachish and Jerusalem were part of a large invasion of Judah. The following passage from the Assyrian king's own records summarizes the campaign.

As for Hezekiah the Jew, who did not submit to my yoke [control], 46 of his strong walled cities, as well as the small cities in their neighbourhood which were without number—by escalade [climbing scaling ladders] and by bringing up siege-engines, by attacking and storming on foot, by mines [saps dug under the walls], tunnels, and breaches, I besieged and took: 200,150 people great and small, male and female, horses, mules, asses, camels, cattle and sheep without number, I brought away from them and counted as spoil.

Quoted in Daniel D. Luckenbill, ed., *Ancient Records of Assyria and Babylonia*, vol. 2. New York: Greenwood, 1989, pp. 120–21.

A relief from the palace of Assyrian king Sennacherib depicts his forces attacking the Hebrew city of Lachish in 701 B.C. Soldiers used a ramped battering ram and ladders to reach the city's hilltop fortification.

mound. This made it impractical, if not impossible, to bring up battering rams and siege towers. Seeing the difficulty of the situation, Sennacherib used a different approach. He ordered his soldiers to build an enormous earthen ramp that approached the front of the stronghold at a gradually increasing upward angle. Once the ramp was in place, the attackers were able to pull up their battering

Remnants of the walled Hebrew city of Lachish, which was defeated by the Assyrians in 701 B.C., can be found in modern-day Israel.

ram, which was protected by a wooden framework covered by animal hides.

While the ram was pounding at a section of the city's defensive wall, Assyrian soldiers climbed scaling ladders they had propped up against the walls. The royal reliefs show them protecting themselves by holding large shields (made of thick layers of wicker) above their heads as they move upward. The sculptures also offer a glimpse inside the town. There, the defenders constructed a huge ramp of their own, intended to reinforce the section of wall that had been weakened by the enemy battering ram.

Although the people of Lachish struggled heroically, their city eventually fell to the Assyrians. Sennacherib also besieged another Hebrew city, Jerusalem. According to the biblical account:

> Sennacherib, king of Assyria, who was besieging Lachish with all his forces, sent his servants to Jerusalem to Hezekiah, king of Judah, [saying,] "On what are you relying, that you stand siege in Jerusalem. . . . Do you not know what I and my fathers have done to all the peoples of other lands?"⁵⁶

Fortunately for the Hebrews, the Assyrian assault on Jerusalem failed. However, in 589 B.C. the Babylonians besieged and captured the city, having prosecuted a successful siege of Lachish the year before.

The Persians also conducted sieges of fortified towns in various sectors of the Near East. In large degree, they modeled their siege devices and tactics on those of the Assyrians. In his famous history book, Herodotus tells how, in 494 B.C., King Darius I besieged the Greek city of Miletus during the rebellion the Anatolian Greeks had launched against the Persian Empire five years before. The Greek historian records the most common outcome of successful Assyrian and Persian sieges—enslaving some of the surviving defenders and deporting the rest back to Mesopotamia:

> [The Persians besieged] Miletus by land and sea. They dug saps under the walls, brought up rams of all kinds, and, five years after the revolt [had begun] overwhelmed it. So Miletus was reduced to slavery. . . . Most of the [Milesian] men were killed by the Persians [and] the women and children were made slaves, and [the] the men in the city whose lives were spared were sent as prisoners to Susa [one of the Persian capitals]. Darius . . . settled them in Ampe, on the Persian Gulf, near the mouth of the Tigris.⁵⁷

Greek Sieges in the Near East

Though the Assyrians, Babylonians, and Persians used siege technology with considerable success, their efforts were later eclipsed in ingenuity and sheer size by those of the Greeks. When Alexander the Great invaded the Persian realm in the 330s B.C., he besieged several cities that offered resistance. The most renowned of these operations was the spectacular siege of the city of Tyre, then subject to the Persians, in 332 B.C.

Alexander's successful capture of Tyre was accomplished by siege devices larger and more advanced than any used previously in Mesopotamia and other parts of the Near East. Among these were large mechanical crossbows, each attached to a wooden framework equipped with a metal winch that slowly drew back the bowstring. These machines unleashed huge arrowlike projectiles that badly damaged the city's battlements. The siege towers used in Greek sieges had large wooden gangways that dropped onto the rooftops of buildings within a city. Soldiers ran down the gangways and quickly took control of the buildings. Greek inventors also created torsion-powered catapults, in which bundles of animal tendons or human hair were twisted tightly and suddenly released, sending massive rocks and other projectiles hurtling as far as .5 mile (.8km) or more. Needless to say, these missiles did horrific damage to stone walls, not to mention the mud-brick houses clustered behind the walls.

In the centuries immediately following Alexander's death in 323 B.C., new generations of Greek inventors, engineers, and machinists produced even more effective and deadly siege technology. The Greek Seleucids, who ruled Mesopotamia beginning in the late fourth century B.C., used these devices. So did the Romans, who invaded Mesopotamia several times in the centuries that followed. In this way, perhaps inevitably, Mesopotamian technology came full circle with disastrous effects. Concepts and devices that had been invented or perfected in the region many centuries before were now used by outsiders to destroy the crumbling remnants of its once great civilization.

Notes

Introduction: Simple but Revolutionary Technology

1. Samuel N. Kramer, *History Begins at Sumer*. Philadelphia: University of Pennsylvania Press, 1981, p. 75.
2. Kramer, *History Begins at Sumer*, p. 75.
3. Daniel C. Snell, *Life in the Ancient Near East, 3100–332 B.C.* New Haven, CT: Yale University Press, 1998, p. 120.

Chapter One: Astronomy, Math, and Measurement

4. Stephen Bertman, *Handbook to Life in Ancient Mesopotamia*. New York: Facts On File, 2003, p. 170.
5. Gwendolyn Leick, *The Babylonians*. London: Routledge, 2003, p. 22.
6. H.W.F. Saggs, *Civilization Before Greece and Rome*. New Haven, CT: Yale University Press, 1991, p. 225.
7. Quoted in Georges Roux, *Ancient Iraq*. New York: Penguin, 1993, p. 334.
8. Gwendolyn Leick, *Historical Dictionary of Mesopotamia*. Lanham, MD: Scarecrow, 2003, p. 132.

Chapter Two: Medicine and Doctors

9. Quoted in Saggs, *Civilization Before Greece and Rome*, p. 263.

10. Quoted in Saggs, *Civilization Before Greece and Rome*, p. 257.
11. A. Leo Oppenheim, *Ancient Mesopotamia: Portrait of a Dead Civilization*. Chicago: University of Chicago Press, 1977, p. 292.
12. Quoted in Joan Oates, *Babylon*. London: Thames and Hudson, 1986, p. 182.
13. Quoted in Oppenheim, *Ancient Mesopotamia*, p. 302.
14. Quoted in Oates, *Babylon*, p. 181.
15. Quoted in Roux, *Ancient Iraq*, p. 370.
16. Quoted in A. Leo Oppenheim, ed., *Letters from Mesopotamia: Official, Business, and Private Letters on Clay Tablets from Two Millennia*. Chicago: University of Chicago Press, 1967, p. 167.
17. Quoted in Richard Hooker, ed., "Mesopotamia: The Code of Hammurabi," World Civilizations, Washington State University, 1996. www.wsu.edu/~dee/MESO/CODE.HTM.
18. Quoted in Hooker, ed., "Mesopotamia."
19. Quoted in Hooker, ed., "Mesopotamia."
20. Quoted in James B. Pritchard, ed., *Ancient Near Eastern Texts Relating to the Old Testament*. Princeton, NJ: Princeton University Press, 1992, pp. 100–101.

21. Karen R. Nemet-Nejat, *Daily Life in Ancient Mesopotamia.* Peabody, MA: Hendrickson, 1998, p. 79.

Chapter Three: Architecture and Building Methods

22. Bertman, *Handbook to Life in Ancient Mesopotamia,* p. 186.
23. Quoted in Gwendolyn Leick, *Mesopotamia: The Invention of the City.* New York: Penguin, 2001, p. 228.
24. Leick, *Mesopotamia,* p. 227.
25. Bertman, *Handbook to Life in Ancient Mesopotamia,* p. 190.
26. L. Sprague de Camp, *The Ancient Engineers.* New York: Ballantine, 1995, p. 26.
27. Leick, *Mesopotamia,* p. 8.
28. De Camp, *The Ancient Engineers,* p. 137.
29. Quoted in Daniel D. Luckenbill, ed., *Ancient Records of Assyria and Babylonia,* vol. 1. New York: Greenwood, 1989, pp. 182–83.
30. Herodotus, *The Histories,* trans. Aubrey de Sélincourt. New York: Penguin, 2003, p. 116.
31. Herodotus, *The Histories,* p. 119.

Chapter Four: Agricultural Tools and Early Weapons

32. Oppenheim, *Ancient Mesopotamia,* p. 314.
33. Wolfram von Soden, *The Ancient Orient,* trans. Donald G. Schley. Grand Rapids, MI: William B. Eerdmans, 1994, p. 98.
34. Saggs, *Civilization Before Greece and Rome,* p. 198.
35. Saggs, *Civilization Before Greece and Rome,* p. 198.
36. Quoted in Sir John Hackett, ed., *Warfare in the Ancient World.* New York: Facts On File, 1990, p. 23.
37. Quoted in Hackett, *Warfare in the Ancient World,* p. 19.

Chapter Five: Advances in Weapons Technology

38. Quoted in Hackett, *Warfare in the Ancient World,* p. 28.
39. Simon Anglim et al., *Fighting Techniques of the Ancient World, 3000 B.C.–A.D. 500.* New York: Thomas Dunne, 2002, p. 82.
40. Arthur Cotterell, *Chariot: The Astounding Rise and Fall of the World's First War Machine.* New York: Overlook, 2005, p. 1.
41. Christon I. Archer et al., *World History of Warfare.* Lincoln: University of Nebraska Press, 2002, p. 4.
42. Archer et al., *World History of Warfare,* p. 4.
43. Anglim et al., *Fighting Techniques of the Ancient World,* p. 83.
44. Quoted in Hackett, *Warfare in the Ancient World,* p. 43.
45. Mark Healy, *The Warrior Pharaoh: Rameses II and the Battle of Qadesh.* Oxford: Osprey, 2000, p. 76.

Chapter Six: Ships and Naval Technology

46. Bertman, *Handbook to Life in Ancient Mesopotamia,* p. 252.

47. Quoted in Hooker, ed., "Mesopotamia."
48. Herodotus, *The Histories,* pp. 119–20.
49. Lionel Casson, *The Ancient Mariners.* Princeton, NJ: Princeton University Press, 1991, pp. 69–70.
50. Herodotus, *The Histories,* p. 393.
51. Barry Strauss, *The Battle of Salamis: The Naval Encounter That Saved Greece and Western Civilization.* New York: Simon and Schuster, 2004, p. 207.

Chapter Seven: Fortifications and Siege Technology

52. Anglim et al., *Fighting Techniques of the Ancient World,* pp. 179–80.
53. Quoted in Hackett, *Warfare in the Ancient World,* p. 16.
54. Peter Connolly, *Greece and Rome at War.* London: Greenhill, 1998, p. 274.
55. Quoted in Hackett, *Warfare in the Ancient World,* p. 48.
56. Second Chronicles 30:10–13.
57. Herodotus, *The Histories,* pp. 394–95.

Glossary

ammatu (or cubit): A Babylonian unit of length measuring 15.5 inches (39cm).

archer pair: In ancient Mesopotamia, a battlefield unit consisting of a shield bearer and an archer.

ard: An ancient Mesopotamian plow.

ashipu: In ancient Mesopotamia, a doctor who used spiritual or magical cures.

asu: In ancient Mesopotamia, a doctor who used natural remedies to heal.

Attic foot: A Greek unit of length used for a while in Mesopotamia, equal to 11.6 inches (29cm).

celestial: Having to do with the sky or heavens.

composite bow: A bow constructed of several different elements that give it more power than an ordinary bow.

coracle: A round reed basket waterproofed on the bottom.

corbelling: Stacking bricks or stones so that each course slightly overhangs the one below.

cosmogony: The study of the universe's origins.

cosmology: The study of the universe and its structure.

exorcism: A religious ritual intended to drive an evil spirit from a person's body.

imeru: In ancient Mesopotamia, a donkey load, equal to about 2.25 bushels.

kelek: A small boat consisting of a wooden frame covered by animal hides.

lunar: Having to do with the Moon.

monumental architecture: Large-scale architecture.

omen: A divine sign indicating that something good or bad will happen.

pier: A vertical support, for instance a pillar.

post and lintel: A basic architectural unit featuring two upright supports topped by a horizontal beam.

retrograde: Backward.

sap: In a siege, a tunnel dug below the enemy fort or city walls.

seed plow: A plow equipped with a funnel that feeds seeds directly into the furrows as the plow moves along; also known as a sowing plow.

sexagesimal system: A mathematical system based on the number 60.

shaduf: A mechanical device for lifting water from one level to another.

shiklu **(or shekel):** A Babylonian unit of weight equaling .3 ounce (9g).

siege: The encirclement and capture of a castle, walled city, or other fortified place.

siegecraft: The skill or art of prosecuting sieges.

solar: Having to do with the Sun.

stade: A unit of length equal to 600 Attic feet.

technology: The application of scientific principles to tools, work, industry, and/or commercial activities.

threshing sled: A device designed to separate wheat grains from the stalks; also known as a threshing board.

trepanation: A medical procedure in which part of the skull is removed.

trireme: An ancient warship featuring three banks of rowers.

ziggurat: A large, pyramid-like structure common in ancient Mesopotamia.

Time Line

B.C.

ca. 9000
Agriculture begins in the Fertile Crescent, the area lying along the western and northern rims of the Mesopotamian plains.

ca. 9000–8000
Stone fortifications, including a tall guard tower, are erected in the Palestinian town of Jericho.

ca. 7500–7000
The earliest known copper items are fashioned in Mesopotamia.

ca. 5000–4000
A wooden plow (*ard*) is introduced in Mesopotamia.

ca. 3300–3000
The Sumerians begin building the world's first cities.

ca. 3000
The first known medical text is written in the Sumerian city of Nippur.

ca. 2000
An unknown Babylonian scribe writes a version of the famous epic poem about the early Mesopotamian hero Gilgamesh.

early 2000s
The seed plow is introduced in Mesopotamia.

ca. 1792–1750
The reign of the Babylonian king Hammurabi, whose famous law code contains statutes relating to doctors and surgery.

ca. 722–705
The reign of Sargon II, under whom Assyria attains its maximum territorial extent.

ca. 700–600
A lunar calendar of twelve months is established in Mesopotamia.

ca. 704–681
The reign of the Assyrian king Sennacherib, who erects the Palace Without Rival and lays siege to the Hebrew cities of Lachish and Jerusalem.

ca. 695
King Sennacherib orders Phoenician warships to be built and transported into Mesopotamia.

ca. 680–669
The reign of the Assyrian king Esarhaddon, whose spiritual advisers recommended exorcism to cure illness.

ca. 668–627
The reign of the last Assyrian monarch, Ashurbanipal, whose library contained some eight hundred medical texts.

ca. 550
Cyrus II, Persia's first king, captures the Median capital of Ecbatana.

480
The Persian king Xerxes attacks Greece, whose city-states eventually repel the invaders.

ca. 400–300
The Babylonian scholar Kidinnu calculates the solar year with an error of only four minutes.

334
The Macedonian Greek king Alexander the Great begins his swift conquest of the Persian Empire.

A.D.
634–651
Muslim Arab armies conquer Mesopotamia and other parts of the Near East, bringing the region's ancient era to a close.

For More Information

Books

Stephen Bertman, *Handbook to Life in Ancient Mesopotamia*. New York: Facts On File, 2003. A fact-filled, easy-to-read guide to the region's peoples, arts and crafts, architecture, science, technology, warfare, and much more.

L. Sprague de Camp, *The Ancient Engineers*. New York: Ballantine, 1995. Reprinted many times, this remains a classic study of ancient technology and devices used for building and warfare.

Lionel Casson, *The Ancient Mariners*. Princeton, NJ: Princeton University Press, 1991. The best available general study of ancient ships and naval technology.

Arthur Cotterell, *Chariot: The Astounding Rise and Fall of the World's First War Machine*. New York: Overlook, 2005. An informative and entertaining examination of one of the more important examples of ancient military technology.

Giovanni Curatola et al., *The Art and Architecture of Mesopotamia*. New York: Abbeville, 2007. A well-illustrated volume that covers all the major examples of ancient Sumerian, Babylonian, and Assyrian art.

John Farndon, *Mesopotamia*. London: Dorling Kindersley, 2007. A beautifully illustrated survey of ancient Mesopotamian history, culture, and life, accessible to readers of all ages.

Gwendolyn Leick, *Mesopotamia: The Invention of the City*. New York: Penguin, 2001. A detailed examination of life in key Mesopotamian cities, including much about architecture and building.

Don Nardo, *The Assyrian Empire*. San Diego: Lucent, 1998. Covers all the major Assyrian rulers and conquests during their three periods of imperial expansion as well as their extensive building projects, military organization, weapons, and conquests.

Karen R. Nemet-Nejat, *Daily Life in Ancient Mesopotamia*. Peabody, MA: Hendrickson, 1998. One of the more comprehensive sources on the subject presently available.

John M. Russell, *Sennacherib's Palace Without Rival at Nineveh*. Chicago: University of Chicago Press, 1992. An excellent exploration of this once magnificent structure, including modern excavations of its ruins.

H.W.F. Saggs, *Civilization Before Greece and Rome*. New Haven, CT: Yale University Press, 1991. This excellent book, by a renowned scholar, contains much information about ancient Mesopotamian science, mathematics, and medicine.

Web Sites

Ancient Mesopotamia: Archaeology (http://oi.uchicago.edu/OI/MUS/ED/TRC/MESO/archaeology.html). This site, run by the famed Oriental Institute of the University of Chicago, features several links to brief but excellent articles about ancient Mesopotamia.

Mesopotamia: The Code of Hammurabi (www.wsu.edu/~dee/MESO/CODE.HTM). This is a good translation of the famous Babylonian ruler's laws. It is part of the World Civilizations Web site hosted by Washington State University.

The Siege of Lachish (www.mesopotamia.co.uk/warfare/story/sto_set.html). The British Museum hosts this site, which tells the story of the Assyrian siege of the Palestinian city of Lachish using a series of Web pages, including photos of ancient sculptures and inscriptions.

Index

Venus tablets, 16, 17
Veterinarians, 32
Volume, 22

W
War chariots, 57, 59–66
Warfare
    cavalry, 65–66
    heavy infantry, 53–55
    methods and tactics, 49–52, 59
    naval, 67–68, 72–77
    siege, 78, 81–88
    transformation of, 11
    See also Weapons
Warships, 67–68, 72–77
Washing methods, 47
Water movers, 44
Watkins, Trevor, 49, 54, 58, 81
Weapons
    advances in, 56–66
    bronze, 56
    chariots, 59–66

    composite bow, 57–59
    metal, 11, 49–51
    missile, 51–52
    stone, 45, 49
Weights and measures, 20–23
West, advanced technology in, 8
Wheels, 9, 11, 61
Wiseman, D.J., 62–63, 82–83
Wood, 38
Woodworking methods, 61
Worldview, 13, 16
Writing, invention of, 9, 10, 18
Wrought iron, 49

X
Xenophon, 62
Xerxes (king), 76

Z
Ziggurats, 40–41, 42
Zimri-Lim (king), 28–29, 40
Zodiac, 16

Picture Credits

About the Author

Historian and award-winning writer Don Nardo has published many books about the ancient world, including *Life in Ancient Athens; The Etruscans; Life of a Roman Gladiator; Religion in Ancient Egypt;* literary companions to the works of Homer, Sophocles, and Euripides; histories of the Assyrian and Persian empires; and Greenhaven Press's encyclopedias of ancient Greece, ancient Rome, and Greek and Roman mythology. He lives with his wife, Christine, in Massachusetts.